1 MONTH OF
FREE
READING

at
www.ForgottenBooks.com

By purchasing this book you are eligible for one month membership to ForgottenBooks.com, giving you unlimited access to our entire collection of over 1,000,000 titles via our web site and mobile apps.

To claim your free month visit:
www.forgottenbooks.com/free920909

ISBN 978-0-265-99763-5
PIBN 10920909

This book is a reproduction of an important historical work. Forgotten Books uses state-of-the-art technology to digitally reconstruct the work, preserving the original format whilst repairing imperfections present in the aged copy. In rare cases, an imperfection in the original, such as a blemish or missing page, may be replicated in our edition. We do, however, repair the vast majority of imperfections successfully; any imperfections that remain are intentionally left to preserve the state of such historical works.

Toronto Philatelic Journal.

VOL. II.   TORONTO, MARCH, 1886.   No. 1.

Record of New Issues.

Any information our readers can give us at any time, regarding recent emissions or changes, will be gratefully received and credited.

AZORES.—The 25r. lilac and 300r. green, have the surcharge in small letters.

BELGIUM has lately brought out three new values, the design of the latest value may be seen in the illustration. 20 centimes, olive; 50c., bistre, and 2 francs, violet.

CEYLON. — Two cards for the Postal Union have been issued, 5c. blue, and 10c. brown.

CONGO —On January 1st, the following values were issued for use in this new African State :— 5 centimes, green; 10c., rose, (see cut); 25c., blue; 50c., green, and postal card 15c., red-brown.

LIBERIA.—The new stamps are of three types. The first has large figure of value in hexagon, with "Republic—Postage—Liberia" at the sides and top, and value below. 1c., carmine; 2c., green; 3c., lilac; 4c., brown; 6c., gray. The second has figure of value on what looks like an egg in the centre, and the same inscription as in type 1, but on fancy scrolls: 8c., blue; 16c., orange. The third has view of a ship and rising sun, with plough and palm tree in the foreground, "Thirty-two" above and "Cents" below on scrolls. Color, dark blue.

MOZAMBIQUE.—A new set of stamps has been issued, values as follows :—5 reis, black; 10r., green; 20r., carmine; 25r., lilac; 40r., brown; 50r., blue; 100r., red brown; 200r., violet; 300r., orange.

PERSIA.—The 5 sh. areen of 1882 and the 10c. carmine are surcharged $\{^{Officia:}_{6}\}$ and $|^{Official}_{12}|$ respectively in black, not for official purposes but for international correspondence.

PERU has lately given birth to two more horrid looking stamps unperforated, and of the values of 5c., blue, and 10c., brown; (see cut), the former bearing the likeness of Admiral Gran, the latter of General Bologneci.

PORTUGUESE INDIA.—There is a new series similar to that noted for Mozambique inscribed "India Portugueza" 1½ reis, black; 4½ reis, brown; 6 reis, green; 1 tanga, carmine; 2 tanga, blue; 4 tanga, lilac; 8 tanga, orange.

PUTTIALLA.—The 4a. has been seen with surcharge in *black* and *red*.

ROUMANIA—Mr. Eugene Brown has received from a correspondent, a 50 bani adhesive of a stone color.

STRAITS SETTLEMENTS.—The 32c. is surcharged "Three cents" in black and there is a reply card 3x3 c. blue on buff.

TRANSVAAL.—A new 2c. stamp has been emitted, brown on white, current pattern.

VICTORIA.— *Der Philatelist* reports the 3d. orange of 1870 and 4d. carmine of 1881, with black surcharge "Stamp Duty."

WESTERN AUSTRALIA.—It is reported that an entire new set of stamps is in course of preparation for this Colony.

UNITED STATES.—Something new. A stamped letter sheet is to be issued soon, combining the letter and envelope in one.

A POSTAGE-STAMP STORY.

Primarily I am a postage stamp ; just a common, every day, two-cent stamp, possessing only such attributes as are peculiar to my class. Indeed, if I were placed among a thousand of my brethren I doubt if the keenest observer would be able to point me out as being in any way distinguished. A vague gloom enshrouds that portion of my life preceding its development into one of the government agents (if I may so call myself) ; and I indistinctly remember having once been connected in some way with a copy of an English comic paper which drifted as an exchange into an American newspaper office, and thence quickly into a huge waste basket. From that time until arriving at my present state, I passed through the hands of paper-dealers, paper manufacturers, and divers clerks and careless people, my last distinct impression being received from an engraver's press.

I can scarcely be called a conceited person ; still I am led to believe that my mission in the world is an important one. I am kind-hearted, of agreeable disposition and well satisfied with my lot. I frequently congratulate myself upon the good fortune which made me what I am. How much better to be, perchance, the bearer of some kind letter, a perfumed billet-doux, if you please, than a vulgar revenue stamp, fit only to adorn a box of ill smelling cigars or grace a barrel of inferior liquor.

A man hurriedly places a postage stamp upon a letter, which he drops in a convenient letter box, and entirely forgets the circumstance. It humbly serves his purpose ; beyond that he does not care. But think for a moment of the travels of that same stamp, of the persons it meets, of the message it bears, and say it is not a sentient being.

After my birth I was carefully accounted for to various commonplace officials, and, after some delay, sent to the postoffice of a certain eastern city. I was purchased soon afterward by Archibald Warrack, who tore me rudely from my friends, and after carrying me about in his pocket-book for a day or two, cast me into a certain dark drawer of hisdesk.

This Mr. Warrack was about 25, tall, graceful and altogether a very gentlemanly appearing person. He dressed neatly and tastefully, but with no suggestion of foppishness. To be frank, I admired him from the beginning of our acquaintance. Regarding his social and financial status, he was a gentleman of artistic tastes—one of the grand army of dilletanti—possessing an ample bank account and a pedigree which was never questioned.

The desk, into a drawer of which I was so ignominiously thrust, stood in a sunny alcove separated from Mr. Warrack's studio by a heavy portiere. This little apartment was a very pleasant place, and Mr. Warrack spent considerable more time in lounging than he did in working in the great, bare room adjoining. Art was a hobby of mine, and it was with much satisfaction that I found myself placed in such a congenial atmosphere.

Soon after being transferred to the drawer I have before alluded to, I discovered that my quarters were shared by a number of other persons of my own kind, who were reposing on dainty perfumed envelopes. There were, however, black stains upon their escutcheons which showed them to be forever ruined. I made bold to introduce myself to one of these scarred veterans, and, after a few preliminary remarks concerning the weather, politics and so on, said :

" From your looks (date of cancelling) I infer that you have been dwelling with this Mr. Warrack for some time, and, being a stranger, I shall esteem it a favor if you will tell me such things as you feel at liberty to speak of concerning his private history."

" It's a sad case," said my friend, with a deep sigh. He looked haggard and worn, and was apparently in great distress.

" How sad ?" I inquired sympathetically.

" A sad case," he continued, without heeding my interruption. " Less than six months ago I was the carrier of a letter, written by a young lady named Rariden—Miss Helen Rariden—to Mr. Warrack, the gentleman whose acquaintance you have recently made. This letter was written in reply to one from 'him in which he exhausted all the available adjectives of the English language in the sincerest avowals of love, closing with an offer of his heart and hand."

" And the letter of which you were the bearer contained—"

"Her acceptance," he said, completing my sentence. "Helen Rariden is a beautiful woman, gifted, wealthy and of excellent family. At the time I parted from her, or rather at the time she parted from me, she loved this—fellow with all her pure soul—loved him as a man was never loved before ; and he doubtless cared for her—then."

The emphasis of this last word was destroyed by a pitiful sob, and for a few moments my friend was so moved that he could not speak. I waited patiently until he again began :

"Shortly after the engagement, which naturally followed, Helen (I take the liberty of so calling her) was compelled to accompany her mother to Europe on a trip undertaken in the hope of benefiting the lady's health. The parting of this Mr. Warrack with his promised bride was tender and touching ; I was present at the time in the gentleman's left-hand coat pocket, and felt the beating of Helen's heart with distinctness for a few blissful moments. I admit that it was an embarrassing position for me to occupy, but I could not well withdraw, as I was then very much attached to this letter, as I am now."

I smiled at this little bit of pleasantry, but my neighbor pressed a convenient pen-wiper to his misty eyes and resumed his narrative.

"After Helen went abroad, Warrack was morose and melancholy for a while ; he began several pictures with which to occupy his mind—gloomy conceptions to correspond with his state of feeling. He first began what he called 'Arthur and Guinevere'—the parting scene, you know. He sketched and daubed at it for a week or so, but kicked it off the easel one day in a fit of impatience. When Helen's first letter came to him (they are in the next drawer below, embellished with cold, haughty, foreign stamps) he replied promptly and at great length—tender, loving messages. O, how true he was l"

The stamp smiled bitterly.

"But he soon became neglectful and would toss Helen's notes into a corner of the desk and not even open them. Of course, under these circumstances, Helen did not write so often, and I soon began to notice a change in Warrack's manner. He became cheerful and planned some joyous pictures ; one of them, a 'Spring' landscape, is on his easel now, and he has ordered the canvas primed for a contemplated work to be called, 'The Lifting of the Clouds.' "

"And what is the cause of this sudden change ?" I asked.

"He is interested in another direction," was the reply.

"And what of Helen ?' I inquired.

"She is still true," answered my friend in a tone of conviction.

This ended our conversation for the time being. My fellow lodger drew back into a dark corner and remained silent for several days.

In the meantime Mr. Warrack seemed happy ; he spent much time in singing and whistling snatches of tunes, chiefly from light operas. He painted when in the right mood and I observed through the keyhole of the drawer that the "Lifting of the Clouds" was progressing finely. It was with pain I thought there might be some connection between the title of the picture and the growing coldness in the manner of the young people towards one another, judging from the dwindling of their correspondence.

A few days after my conversation with the elderly stamp, Mr. Warrack opened our drawer and threw in an unopened letter which he had just received. As soon as he went out my friend snatched it and examined it eagerly. The envelope bore the card of a Venetian hotel and a cancelled postage stamp whose language we did not know.

"From Helen ?" I said, interrogatively.

"Yes," was the mournful reply.

Time wore on. It is a fashion time has, even in the life of lowly postage stamps. Spring came tripping down her bright, flower malled path, and in the darkness of our habitation we felt the stirring of re-awakened life. Mr. Warrack did not enter his studio for days at a time. When I spoke of these long absences to my chum he only answered in the language of Tennyson :

In the spring a livelier iris changes on the burnished dove ;
In the spring a young man's fancy lightly turns to thoughts of love.

Continued on page 8.

TORONTO

PฅILATELIC JOᴜRNALᒆ

Published on the 15th of every month.

SUBSCRIPTION PRICE.

United States and Canada, 25 cents a year; Foreign
Countries, 35 cents.

ADVERTISING RATES.

Per inch,	-	-	.	-	-	$ 50
Per half inch,	.	:	.	.	.	30
Per column,	.	.	.	.	-	2 75
Per half column,	-	.	.	.	-	1 50
Per page,	-	-	.	-	-	5 0ɔ

Twenty per cent. discount given on standing advertisements of over three months.
All advertisements must be in by the 10th of the month
to insure insertion in the same number.

TERMS STRICTLY CASH IN ADVANCE.

Except amounts under $1.00, which may be remitted
in one and two cent stamps.
Address all communications to

H. MORELL,

Editor and Publisher,

76 BALDWIN ST., TORONTO, CANADA.

We are pleased to present to the philatelic
public the first number of volume two of the
TORONTO PPILATELIC .JOURNAL, which, it
will be noticed is vastly improved in size and
style.

During the twelve months of its existence
the TORONTO PHILATELIC JOURNAL has
changed hands more than once, but we find
in looking over the volume that the style and
manner of conducting it has been pretty
much the same, its circulation has been uniform each month, and our subscription books
alone show that collectors appreciate it.

Advertisers also know the value of the
JOURNAL as a medium hence our increased
size which we shall endeavor to make as interesting if not more so than formerly. With
increasing the size and get up we have not
increased the subscription nor advertising
rates. Sample copies will be mailed free to
any address.

Why is a sheet of perforated postage stamps
like distant relations? Because they are but
slightly connected.

The Stamp Collectors of Altoona, Pa.,
organized a society under the name of
"Altoona .Philatelic Society." Officers are
as follows : W. R. Fraser, president ; E. C.
Mann, secretary, and Edw. E. Kendig, treasurer. We wish it success.

Mr. C. E. Swope of Messrs. C. E. Swope
& Co'y. has purchased Mr. C. B. Norton's
interest in the firm and will hereafter conduct the business himself and will carry it on
in his own name.

We hereby warn the Philatelic public that
J. A. Webb and B. De Witt Opry of Atlanta,
Ga., are frauds of the deepest dye. Mr.
Whilden informs us that they are one and
the same party and these are assumed names.
Their ads. appeared in this paper : parties
who answered their advertisements in this
Journal and did not receive satisfactory
returns, will do well to communicate with the
publisher, also stating date of sending and
amount of money enclosed.

MR. GEORGE A LOWE, LATE the
well-known Editor of the "TORONTO PHILA-
TELIC JOURNAL," has just disposed of his
whole stock of valuable STAMPS, including
many varieties of Canada, United States, Newfoundland, &c., &c., and of his entire business
and valuable connection to MESSRS. GAED-
ECHEN & CO., 248 Mare Street, London,
and MR. WM. BROWN, Riverside, Castle
Street, Salisbury, and who, with their own
stock of valuable and most rare STAMPS,
extending over a variety of 9000, are able to
execute any orders from the most advanced
Collectors and Dealers, and at prices which
are acknowledged by the trade to be lower
than those of any other respectable and leading dealer.

" It isn't the salary I care for," said the
applicant for the Squashville post-office; "but
my wife and daughters are mighty anxious to
read the postal cards that pass through the
mails."

General Logan's mail is, taking the year
round, probably the largest of any member
in either branch of Congress. It frequently
exceeds 200 letters a day, and seldom falls
below 150.

Among Our Exchanges.

We desire to exchange with every paper in the world published in the interest of, or having a department pertaining to Philately.

Publishers, please send us two (2) copies of your paper each month, and we will be pleased to reciprocate.

The Stamp is a very neat little paper from Denver, Colorado, it contains a good article on surcharges.

The Stamp and Coin Gazette is the same as usual "up to the mark." It is now one of the best stamp papers published.

The Philatelic Magazine for February comes to hand with twelve pages of well-written philatelic literature. Keep on Mr. Bishop, you are doing very well.

The Philatelic Exchange List is a new one from England, it "comes out" with eight pages and well filled with very fair reading matter. We wish you success Mr. Bishop.

The Philatelic News, volume one, number one to hand, it promises to be a leading paper.

The National Capital Philatelist, number two, is at hand. It has enlarged to about double the size of number one. March number will be enlarged to double the size of number two, "it is doing well in this climate."

We have also received the following papers, publishers accept thanks : Empire State Philatelist, Youth's Ledger, Wayne Times, Collectors' Journal, Capital City Philatelist, Philatelic Tribune, Tidings from Nature, The Exchange, Long Island Collector, The Wyoming Cactus, British Philatelist, The Stamp Dealers' Journal, Arizona Pride of Philately, Genius of Youth, West American Scientist, The Observer, Stamp Collectors' Journal, The Chenung Review.

THE OREGON'S MAIL.

About two thousand three hundred registered letters and a very heavy general mail were in the ship. Of the closed mails not received there were the following letter bags : —For New York, 110 ; Philadelphia, 8 : St. Louis, 7 ; Chicago, 3 ; San Francisco, 2 ; Ottawa, 4 ; Montreal, 5 ; Toronto, 5 ; Hamilton, 5 ; Quebec, 4 ; Kingston, 5 ; Halifax, 2 ; St. John, N. B., 3 : Prince Edward Island, 3 ; Winnipeg, 3.

ANNO DOMINI 1885.

A gloomy and somewhat dispiriting review of the past year, considered from a Philatelist's point of view, has quite recently appeared in a contemporary, and it is seriously stated that Stamp Collecting is on the decline. How far this may be true, I cannot, at present, give any opinion. My purpose, in the present article, is to take into consideration some of the various causes to which the decline is attributed, and I will take them in their order :—1st—Imprudent circulation of remainders; 2nd–The traffic in forged stamps; and 3rd—Lack of literature bearing on the subject.

The first reason is one which rests entirely with the large dealers. The second is, I believe, steadily on the decline, and I await with interest the promised revelations by one who is said to be behind the scenes. I do not place much, if any, faith in such promises, and I have only got one thing to say, and that is, "produce your revelations!"

Lack of literature bearing on the subject will seem, to a great many, as it is to me, rather a curious reason. We have literature of some sort, presumably devoted to the science, but, with a few exceptions, failing most ignominiously in their declared aims ; and, while on this subject, I may state that it does not pay to publish Stamp papers, and until Collectors are prepared and willing to support publishers, they will never have a respectable number of papers devoted to their hobby. I would strongly advise all intending publishers to ascertain the amount of support they are likely to receive, before embarking in such a hazardous enterprise as catering for the stamp collecting fraternity.—"SPERO MELIORA," in *The Stamp Collectors' Journal.*

Those tiny things called postage stamps which are as light as feathers and might be blown about by the slightest breeze, make up in aggregate very considerable bulk and weight, as will be appreciated when it is mentioned that one year's issue in the United Kingdom amounts to no less than 114 tons.

In Stuttgart, Germany, the tricycle has been adopted by the government for the postal service.

Numismatic Department.

BY J. HOOPER.

All correspondence and information intended for this department should be addressed to J. Hooper, Esq., Box 145, Port Hope, Canada.

The dates of Canadian 50c. pieces are corrected as follows : 1870, 1871 with and without H below wreath 1872 and 1881. In 5c. issue of 1874 two different dies have been used on Reverse, the 4 being plain and crosslet (thus 4). We note a 2 Trade Tokens issued by Dr. Le Roux, of Montreal, as follows.

1. Obv. "Acheter le Canadian Copper Coin Catalogue $0.50 ; L'Atlas Numismatique du Canada $1.50 et $2.00 ; et Le Vade Mecum du Collectionneur $1.00, Par Jos. Le Roux, M. D., Montreal, Canada."
Rev. "Buy the Canadian Coin Catalogue $0.50, Numismatic Atlas for Canada $1.50 and $2.00, and Collectors' Vade Mecum $1.00, by Jos. Le Roux, M. D., Montreal, Canada." Copper and Brass size 16. Struck December, 1885.

2. Obv. "Labor improbus omnia vincit." Arms in quartered shield surmounted by beaver L, olive and laurel branch crossed beneath.
Rev. Same as obverse of No. 1. Copper and Brass, size 16½ struck January, 1886.

The Canadian tokens and medals (discovered by myself during 1885) are as follows :

1. Geo. Burns, clothier, London , Ont.
2. Faucher token, Peterboro, Ont.
3. Father Matthew medal, issued for Kingston, Ont , in 1842. W. M. size 28.
4. Oshawa Knights of Labor Demonstration, August 13th, 1883.
Rev. Joseph Hall Works, Oshawa. Iron, size 40.
5. "Bible Army" on open Bible.
6. Obv. surmounted by beaver and encircled by wreath, " The Dominion must and shall be preserved."
Rev. "W. H. Banfield, Machinist and Die maker, Toronto." W. M., size 21.
7. In Sacramental Tokens.
Eight pointed star, crown in centre surrounded by the words, "Methodist Army." W. M., size 24.
8. Baltimore, C. W., 1855.

9. Cobourg, U. C., 1837.
10. Token of Rev. John Donglas " Cavan" with initials J. D.
11. Obv. Saint Andrew's Church, Quebec, in centre.
Rev. Sacramental token 1821.
13. Rev. John Cassie, sacramental token of Port Hope with initials J. C.
12. In Bank of Upper Canada 1852, 1d. issue, two different dies have been used on the obverse, the difference being very apparent in the numerals being smaller, the Obv. and Rev. being straight in the variety. This feature has never been mentioned as yet by any Canadian Numismatist.
Obv. Beaver on stick of maple, with three leaves. "Montreal, Canada," above, "1886 M. E. L." below.
Rev. "E. A. Cardinal, Numismatist, Montreal," 2 patras. Brass, size 17.
The dies broke before 100 was struck.

The most complete collection of coins in America, embracing coins of every description, from the early Colonial days down to the present time, is in the possession of Loring G. Parmalee, of Boston. Its intrinsic value is something less than $1,200, but its mercantile value is about $70,000.

The Philadelphia mint first began to coin dollars in 1794. This was the first issue of the United States standard silver dollar. The New Orleans mint first coined dollars in 1846, the San Francisco mint in 1859, and the Carson City mint in 1870. The New Orleans mint did no coining from Jan 26, 1861, to Feb. 20, 1879.

On the Chinese coins the obverse bears the name of the reign, and the words "current money." On the reverse is the name of the mint.

An Austrian post-office circular gives a list of 196 newspapers which are forbidden to be transmitted through the post, either by reason of judicial sentence under the press laws or simply under a Ministerial rescript of the Department. Only seven belong to the first-class, three of which are German and four Italian. The remaining 189 papers are excluded from postal circulation for political reasons and simply by an order of the postal authorities.

Exchanges.

In order to facilitate the exchange of duplicates, and with a view to bringing about more intimate relations among collectors, we offer a column per month, *free of charge to our subscribers only*, wherein they may state what they have to dispose of and what they desire in exchange. Notices must be written on a separate sheet of paper.

Wanted, old issue Canadian Stamps. Pence issue specially desired for cash or exchange. Address EDW. Y. PARKER, 12 Orde Street, Toronto, Canada.

50 Sea Shells for every 25 official, 100 revenue or 100 old issue U.S. stamps. WILL M. CLEMENS, Jamestown, N. Y.

U. S. revenue document, match, medicine, proprietary and plain card stamps; also U. S. department and postage stamps to exchange for others of same not n my collection. Correspondence solicited with advanced collectors. A. B. G., P. O. Box 67, Brooklyn, N.Y.

6 West India sea beans for every 200 mixed Canadian Stamps. WILL. M. CLEMENS, Jamestown, N. Y.

15 cents worth of curiosities for every special delivery stamp—those on the original envelope preferred. Send for list of curio. and coins I have to exchange for good postage and revenue stamps. EDW. J. STEBBINS, Adrian, Mich.

Wanted. I want all kinds of war relics, such as swords, bayonets, old pistols, etc., for which I will pay cash or give foreign stamps in exchange. H. MORELL, 76 Baldwin Street, Toronto.

Wanted to exchange.—Two books, viz.: "History of the Lives and Bloody Exploits of the most noted Pirates," and "Daring Deeds of American Generals." ROBERT L. STEPHENS, State Line City, Warren Co., Ind., U.S.

Correspondence desired in the following countries: Transvaal Republic, Orange Free States, and all parts of South America. Address, K. L., (upper left hand corner of envelope); the publisher of this paper.

I wish to exchange with foreign collectors. Correspondence desired. T. J. McMINN, 102 Rose Avenue, Toronto, Canada.

Will exchange all kinds of stamps with advanced collectors. Rare United States stamps especially desired. H. MORELL, 76 Baldwin Street, Toronto, Canada.

Correspondence.

We solicit, and are prepared to insert under this heading, any information or suggestions that may be thought of interest to the Philatelic world. Should anyone wish to have any point explained, upon which their mind is not quite clear, we shall be glad to insert the problem in this department, and in the next number will insert the solutions as given by our readers, so that the questions will be fully answered by different parties, and from different stand points. Those who think they can give any information on any of the subjects inquired about, are cordially invited to give their ideas by writing to the editor of this paper, mentioning the signature to the query, and the communication will be published in the next issue also. We hold ourselves in readiness to give here such information as lies in our power, and are prepared, at all times, to assist Philatelists in the solution of such questions as we are able to.

Chicago.—Remit at once for your six months "ad." if you do not wish to see your name put under the dead beats.

L. Rappleye.—We do not accept stamps in payment for ads.

Edwards, Peeke & Co.'y.—Thanks for your favor.

W. M.—Have nothing to do with them. They are frauds of the worst kind.

Chas. King.—You ask how to make a Stamp Album. The following appeared in March Number of *Youth's Ledger*. Try it.—"A very good stamp album can be made of a good sized blank-book. By the aid of a catalogue or a printed album, borrowed from a brother collector, the blank pages may be ruled for the stamps of each country. A few more spaces should be left than there are existing stamps, for new issues. These blank-books are cheap and can be made to look quite handsome."

H. D., New York.—Communicate with Jos. Hooper, Box 145, Port Hope, Canada. He will be able to inform you.

J. C. H., Belleville.—Originals could not be procured at any such price. The correct price is about one dollar for the four; consequently 10 cents is extra cheap. Better leave them alone.

H.—Please remit.

J. S., Chicago.—Morell's Directory will *not* be sent on approval. Send on twenty-five cents if you wish to receive a copy.

The only thing that can make money without advertising—the mint. So advertise in the *Toronto Philatelic Journal.*

"Poor Helen !" he said.   " O, woman, you alone are long suffering and true."

Spring, summer, and fall.

One bright autumn day, as my friend 'and I were conversing in our quarters, Mr. Warrack, who was sitting in the alcove reading a newspaper, cut from its society columns two items which had, through the instrumentality of Fate and the typographical "make-up," been printed in this order :.

Cards have been issued for the wedding of Mr. Archibald Warrack, the rising young artist, and Miss Florence Springer, daughter of Jay Winter Springer, the poet.

"O, the perfidy of man," said my poor stamp friend when I had finished reading.

The other item read :

A cablegram from Venice announces the marriage at that place of Miss Helen Rariden, who has been sojourning abroad for some time past, to Sir Arthur Lombard, of London.

"The devil !" gasped my friend, through the dust which covered him.

"Not the devil, but the way of the world," said I.

LAST PAGE IN HISTORY OF DEPARTMENT STAMPS.

Written for Toronto Philatelic Journal.

According to the report of Third Assistant Postmaster General (see P. M. General's report page 666) the whole amount of official postage stamps and stamped envelopes issued to the several executive departments, under the Act of March 3rd, 1873, until they were abolished by the Act of July 5th, 1884, represented a value of $8,049,609.09, of which $5,831,460.22 was credited as receipts of the post office ; the balance of $2,138,310.85 representing the amount of stamps used by the Post Office Department in the years of 1877, 1878, and 1879, did not go to the credit of that department, further appropriations for the purpose being denied by Congress. Besides the above in January 1885, there were in the vaults of the stamp contractors $17,024,588 worth of stamps of various denominations ranging from 1c. to $20 which with what had been left over in the various offices were destroyed by burning. So the curtain has rung down over the Department stamps of the United States.   What will the collector of the nineteenth century say about them.   As to the stock destroyed, the New York dealers expected to have a pic-nic out of them but were disappointed. Without an Act of Congress they expected to get them at the cost of printing.

J. H. HOUSTON.

When answering advertisements kindly mention this paper.

— THE —

Toronto Philatelic Journal.

A MONTHLY MAGAZINE

DEVOTED TO THE INTEREST OF STAMP COLLECTORS.

Price 25 Cents Per Annum.

APRIL, 1886.

H. MORELL,

PUBLISHER,

76 Baldwin Street, Toronto, Canada.

✦THE✦
Toronto Philatelic Journal.

| VOL. II. | TORONTO, APRIL, 1886. | No. 2. |

Record of New Issues.

Any information our readers can give us at any time, regarding recent emissions or changes, will be gratefully received and credited.

Bermuda, a post card, 1½d. carmine on buff, has been issued.

British Bechuanaland. For this colony the following values of Cape of Good Hope have been surcharged. ½ penny, ; black, 1 penny, rose ; 2 pence, brown ; 6 pence, violet. See annexed cut.

Ceylon, a new 5c. stamp has been issued, color, lilac, with the head of Victoria to left in oval, " Ceylon " above, " postage " at left, " revenue " at right, and " five cents " below.

Finland. The 10 pennia carmine, is now in use.

Gibraltar. The following new surcharges have appeared. 1 penny, rose ; 2 penny, brown ; 4 pence, orange ; 6 pence, violet ; and 1 sh., light brown, of Bermuda, and ½ penny cards and wrappers of Natal.

Guatemala. *The World* gives the following :—A decree dated February 12th, authorizes a provisional issue of stamps of 25c., 50c., 75c., 100c., 150c. These consist of the stock of stamps used for the payment of the Northern Railway tax. with new value surcharged. They have the portrait of General Barrios in oval band inscribed " Republica de Guatemala." Above on scroll " Ferrocarril al Norte " and below on straight label " Vale un peso." They are large stamps measuring about 24x30 mm. and printed in red (C. C. 123.) Perforated 12. The surcharge is as follows : at top " Correos Nacionales " in the middle " Guatemala " and at the foot the value. The value is also repeated four times at the sides, and there are besides various type set ornaments, in the three lower values links of chains and in the 100 and 150 somewhat like those on the Cuba 1883, but smaller.

Gwalior. The following values have appeared : 1 anna and 6 pies brown ; 3 annas orange ; 6 annas brown.

Reunion Isles. Of the surcharges known to be genuine, are the 5c. on 40c. (Eagle, 5c. on 40c. (Liberty) 5c. on 50c. (Figs of Commerce). 5c. on 30c. (Napoleon laureated), 10c. on 40c. (Figs of Commerce), 25c. on 40c. (Eagle). See illustration.

Santander. This month we illustrate a new type that has been prepared for the three values in use in this state. The colors are unchanged, they being as following : 1 centavo, blue ; 5 centavos, red (see cut) ; 10 centavos, violet.

Tobago. A post card 1 penny has been issued and the 6 pence adhesive, surcharged ½ penny in black.

Tolima. Mr. Bogert chronicles a 20c. stamp lilac. The usual arms are in the centre with "Correos del E.° S.° del Tolima " in two lines in a curved label above, supported by pillars at the sides. At the bottom is " Centavos " and the figures " 20 " in circles in lower corners.

Uruguay. There has been a new post card issued, it is 3x3 green on violet.

Victoria. The three pence orange of 1866 and 4 pence carmine of 1881 have been surcharged "Stamp duty."

ABOUT PIGEON POSTS.

BY WILL M. CLEMENS.

The first well-known and authenticated instance of the use of the carrier pigeon as a means of conveying letters by post was during the siege of Paris in 1870. No mention of the postal affairs of France would be complete without some notice of the pigeon service during the siege. The subject has been written about before, I candidly admit, but the financial side of the question does not seem to be unduly dwelt upon. It is somewhat startling to learn that during the siege of Paris each carrier bird in the postal service carried £11,520 in postage. The rate was in round numbers about four pence per word and there was a registration fee of about twelve cents in United States money.

The postage on letters during the siege sent by pigeon post averaged about one dollar each, so that on two hundred letters sent by this service the post amounted to over $800. The letters were written in groups of two hundred on a screen, and were then photographed down as if for the microscope, on to one of the tiny pages carried by the pigeon. These pages were a sixteenth of each pellicle, so that each pellicle realized sixteen times £40 or £640, and as each pigeon carried eighteen pellicles, we get the total of each bird's mail as worth eighteen times £640 or £11,520, and it was well worth it, considering that a pigeon would sometimes bring in from Tours, as many as 50,000 despatches and that the balloon with the birds had first to make its way out of Paris over the German lines. The men in charge of the balloons had however much to be thankful for, for notwithstanding Krupp's postal guns and various other devices, only seven balloons were captured by the Germans.

At the present time a pigeon post is at daily work in the Fiji Islands. The letters and communications from island to island being carried on by birds. The Fijian exports are chiefly fruits, and as the fruit would spoil if left two long in store, means were necessary to give early notice of when the picking would take place and the news of the arrival of various steamers is now sent out through the colony by pigeon post. Until recently the important telegrams in the English papers were sent by pigeons from Point de Galle to Colombo, seventy miles higher up the coast of Ceylon. In different countries and at different times the carrier pigeon has been a letter carrier ever since the days of Anaceron.

A PERMANENT STAMP ALBUM.

BY W. G. WHILDEN, JR.

At the present time, when the market is flooded with every kind of albums, collectors are sometimes troubled to know which kind is the best. All albums have certain merits. But the following plan, which I have successfully tried myself, is, I think, a method that will please the most fastidious. For collectors of United States stamps exclusively, it is especially adapted. Have an album made about 8½ x 11 inches, containing 48 leaves (96 pages), of the finest quality of white paper, almost as thick as cardboard, with guards between the leaves to give the album the proper appearance. The pages on the left side are to be ruled, while those on the right are to be perfectly blank. The stamps are to be inserted on the blank pages, and a complete description, exact date of issue, etc., should be written on the left. There should be no spaces laid off for the stamps; therefore you can arrange them in any desired way your fancy may suggest. After which a neat border should be ruled around each stamp, to "show it off." If you are very fastidious you might first mount the stamps on rectangular squares of cardboard. This will make them look much better, but of course it will be more troublesome.

In regard to the cost of the album. I would say that it should not cost over $3.00, if it is bound in morocco and gilt. Of course, a cloth binding would do. But a morocco one will look much better, and will not cost very much more.

I know that the above plan is a *good* one by personal experience, and therefore I can recommend it. Some persons prefer the stamps to be mounted, *first*, on a rectangular piece of white, and *second*, on sheets of grey cardboard; but you can use your discretion in the matter. In regard to mounting the stamps according to the last method, a first-rate plan is as follows : Obtain some *pure, refined* gum arabic, and dissolve it in a small quantity of clean, warm water. Dip a *small* sized camel's hair brush in the solution and run it across the top of the stamp. Attach this to the cardboard " mount," which should be securely fastened to the pages of the album, with a piece of gummed paper.

The album described above is a permanent one in every sense of the word, and one that will suit all classes of advanced collectors. It will, of course, take practice to arrange the stamps tastily, but when you have once succeeded you will be proud of it, and you will not be ashamed to show it to your friends and acquaintances.—*The Youth's Ledger.*

STAMP COLLECTING IN THE FUTURE.

BY SPENCER COSBY.

A number of articles have been making the rounds of the philatelic papers with such titles as " Stamp Collecting in 1986," " A Stamp Collector 200 years from now," etc. The idea is nearly the same in all of them, and usually runs about as follows : The philatelist of 1986 or 2086, or of whatever future century he may be, owns a collection numbering anywhere from fifty thousand to one hundred and fifty thousand varieties, contained in a dozen or more folio volumes, and requiring several days to be looked over. His greatest rarity is some such stamp as the two cent U.S. 1883 issue, or the three cent 1870 issue, or some other stamp common perhaps in the 19th century, but whose origin and use is now clothed in obscurity.

Articles of the above nature may be amusing, and indeed I suppose that is their object, as I do not think they give at all a correct idea of what stamp collecting will be in the future. It seems much more probable that as the number of stamps increases, collectors will become specialists and devote their attention to certain branches of philately only. This is the case in numismatics, for we only find young collectors taking coins of all nations and of all ages indiscriminately. By the time that thirty or forty thousand different stamps have been issued the number of collectors will

probably be three or four times as large as it is now, and the value of obsolete stamps will have increased proportionately.   The consequence will be that persons of moderate means and with no great amount of spare time will find it an utter impossibility to obtain a compiete collection, and only dealers who devote their whole time to the business, and persons with plenty of money who make it their hobby will even attempt to collect stamps of all kinds. The great majority of philatelists will take up some branch suited to their means and in which they feel particular interest. Some will only collect the stamps of their own country, others will select certain countries and confine their attention to them, others again will collect only those stamps issued between certain dates.

In fact, although the number of postage stamps that have appeared up to the present day is comparatively small, many collectors have already become specialists, and a movement in that direction seems to have already begun.   In Europe nearly all the advanced philatelists collect all kinds of stamps, postage, revenue, telegraph, postal cards, etc.   In this country very few collectors care for revenues, and those who do keep them separate from their postage stamps.   Postal cards seem also to be generally neglected, and it is only lately that persons have begun to collect envelope stamps on the whole envelope, as many consider them to have lost much of their value if cut from it. There is a large and growing class of collectors who collect only U.S. stamps and some few are beginning to discard all provisionals.

This movement toward becoming specialists will, in all likelihood, steadily continue, and it will not be long before it will be an exception to find a person collecting even all varieties of postage stamps.   Of course this will only be the case if new issues continue to appear as often as they do now, and from present appearances we should judge that they would.   But none of us know what the future may have in store for philately, and indeed in the onward march of invention it is not at all improbable that some new and improved system of prepayment of postage may be devised which will entirely do away with the use of stamps, so that but for collectors their very existence might be forgotten a few centuries hence.—*The Stamp and Coin Gazette.*

TORONTO

PHILATELIC JOURNAL

Published on the 15th of every month.

SUBSCRIPTION PRICE.

United States and Canada, 25 cents a year; Foreign
Countries, 35 cents.

ADVERTISING RATES.

Per inch,	-	-	-	-	-	$ 50
Per half inch,	-	-	-	-	-	30
Per column,	-	-	-	-	-	2 75
Per half column,	-	-	-	-	-	1 50
Per page,	-	-	-	-	-	5 00

Twenty per cent. discount given on standing advertisements of over three months.
All advertisements must be in by the 10th of the month
to insure insertion in the same number.

TERMS STRICTLY CASH IN ADVANCE.

Except amounts under $1.00, which may be remitted
in one and two cent stamps.
Address all communications to

H. MORELL,

Editor and Publisher,

76 BALDWIN ST., TORONTO, CANADA.

Horace C. Jones, of Minneapolis, Minn.,
has turned out to be one of the worst frauds
of the season. He has cheated nearly all the
stamp papers out of money for his advertising,
and those parties who have sent him money
have not received any returns. His advertisement appeared in last month's issue of
this paper. When sending his advertisement
he wrote on a letter head of "The Rector's
Messenger" and referred us to his father, the
publisher of the above paper, Rev. Melville
C. Jones. It has been ascertained that there
is no such a paper published as "The Rector's Messenger," nor is there such a party as
the Rev. Melville C. Jones. The first that
we heard of the affair was the following letter :

GEORGETOWN, MASS., April 4th, 1886.

H. Morell, Esq.,

DEAR SIR,—No 1 of Vol. 2 of your paper to hand
and contents noted. In it is an advertisement of
Horace C. Jones, of Minneapolis, Minn. I received
a letter a few days ago from the P. O. Inspector of
Chicago in which he said that Horace C. Jones had

been complained of as a fraud and wanted to know
if I had sent him goods or money. I am happy to
say I had not. I hope you will warn your subscribers against him.
Yours truly,
FRANK DONOHOE.

THE U. S. SPECIAL DELIVERY.

The special delivery service of the postal
department does not grow in popularity. On
the contrary, the number of letters carried in
the mails under this stamp has grown smaller
every month since the system was started,
and the total for February was only sixty-five
thousand one hundred and fifty-nine, against
eighty-six thousand one hundred and twenty-
three in November. There is nothing strange
about this, for the service has little to recommend it. Anybody who really demands
celerity is pretty sure to prefer the telegraph
or the messenger service, and the possible
field is thus very restricted. Then, too, the
system causes no little inconvenience to re-
cipients of letters. A letter bearing this
stamp, if received at the office at any moment
before midnight, must be delivered that night,
and the result is that people are waked out
of their sleep at half-past twelve or one o'clock
to receive letters which would be brought
around by breakfast-time at the first carrier's
round, and which they do not care about
getting before that time. The amount of
midnight profanity caused by this special-
delivery business in the course of a year is by
no means inconsiderable.

A lady has succeeded in writing two thousand words upon a postal card. Ordinarily
it would require at least five cards to contain
that number of words, which is a clear saving
of four cents towards a new sealskin. But
how few men there are who can appreciate
these little economies in a wife.

The postmaster general has received a letter from Cheyonne, W. T., signed "From a
Christian," containing $140, which the writer
says he stole twenty years ago from two letters in the Peru, Neb., postoffice. An owner
of the $40 has been found at North Platte,
Neb., and search will be made for the owner
of the balance.

Among Our Exchanges.

We desire to exchange with every paper in the world published in the interest of, or having a department pertaining to Philately.

Publishers, please send us two (2) copies of your paper each month, and we will be pleased to reciprocate.

The Philatelic Journal of America has, with the March number, entered into its second volume. It contains a very good article on the Postage Stamps of British Guinea by Jas M. Chute, also a lengthy subject on Confederate Stamps by the well-known writer, R. S. Hatcher.

The Stamp and Coin Gazette is really a first-class paper. Every month it brings out something new, both for philatelists and numismatists.

The Collectors' Science Monthly, Vol 1, No. 1, to hand. It is one of the best journals published. It has illustrations for every department and comes out with twenty pages and cover.

Quaker City Philatelist for March to hand. It contains a very good piece of philatelic poetry by Yum-Yum and full reports of the Q.C.P.S.

Collectors' Companion. The March number contains thirty-two pages and cover and is very interesting from beginning to end. .

The Philatelic Star. In the March number Mr. Herdman goes for the "leading dealers" for not paying cash for their "ads." but gives reprints of stamps to publishers inserting their advertisements.

We have also received the following papers. Publishers please accept thanks: *Monthly Journal, The Chemung Review, Brufmarken-Zeitung-Universum, Deutsche-Brufmarken-Zeitung, Youths' Pilot, Philatelic Tribune, Philatelic Mercury, Philatelic Herald, National Capital Philatelist, Stamp World, Genius of Youth.*

In all 256 bags have thus far been recovered of 598 despatched by the Oregon.

Mr. Lyman H. Lowe has favored us with a copy of "Hard Times Tokens." Collectors of this class of coins would do well to send for a copy of it.

STAMP AUCTION.

An auction sale of foreign and U. S. postage stamps will take place in St. Louis, early in May. The sale will be catalogued by C. H. Mekeel, of the Carson Stamp Co., and Chas. Votier, of the St. Louis Postage Stamp Co. Catalogues may be obtained from either of these parties.

The sale will be of interest to both collectors and dealers, as the catalogue will contain some rarities, as well as some very fine lots of South and Central American stamps, suitable for dealers.

There will also be a lot of foreign postals and revenues offered, and a few U. S. entire envelopes and revenues, among which may be mentioned the rare $200.00 revenue.

The stamps will be sold without reserve, at public auction. Place and date will be named later. Bids will be executed by all St. Louis dealers.

HOW TO TELL FORGED STAMPS.

It is a great shame that stamps should be forged to deceive the young Philatelist, but it is done so much now, and such exact imitations are procured, that it deceives both the young and the old ; but, readers, I am glad to say it is being stopped now.

To find out a forged stamp, see below :—Take a magnifying glass and look at the stamp which you think is a forgery and compare it with another and you will see (if it is a forgery) that the lines are much coarser and the gum at the back is laid on very thick (as a rule) and is more yellowish ; you also find a forged stamp perforated very badly, or not at all. You should then hold the stamp to the light and look for a watermark, as you rarely find one on a forged stamp. Readers, by following the above examples you can keep yourself from buying forged stamps.—C. F. C. in the *Stamp Collectors' Journal.*

Why is a postage stamp like a schoolmaster? Because one sticks with a lick and the other licks with a stick.

There were 7,084 Post Offices in Canada in 1885.

Numismatic Department.

BY J. HOOPER.

All correspondence and information intended for this department should be addressed to J. Hooper, Esq., Box 145, Port Hope, Canada.

CORRECTED DATES OF ISSUE OF NEWFOUNDLAND COINS.

$2, gold, 1865, '70, '72, '80, '81, '82, 85.

50 cents silver, 1870, '72, '73, '74, '76, '80, '81, '82, '85.

20 cents silver, 1865, '70, '72, '73, '76, '80, '81, '82, '85.

10 cents silver, 1865, '70, 72, '73, '76, 80, '82, '85.

5 cents silver, 1865, '70, '72, '73, '76, '80, '81, '82, '85.

1 cent copper, 1865, '70, '72, '73, '76, '80, '85.

The above list of dates are verified by the agent of the Union Bank, St. John's, Newfoundland, in a recent letter to me.

The new issue of 1886, Dominion silver and copper, is making its appearance through the various banks.

W. H. Banfield, machinist and die maker, Toronto, has issued three varieties of bronze medals for distribution at the Colonial Exhibition to be held at London, England, this year. One variety has on Rev. "Exhibition Souvenir," (around outer circle), and the following in three scrolls in centre: "Fish Creek," "Batoche," "Cut Knife." The medals are well got up and reflect credit on the issuer.

The medals to be given to the soldiers, who bravely volunteered and went to the North-West, have arrived in Ottawa and are being engraved with each recipient's name on the edge. A formal presentation will no doubt be given.

In tearing down the old ferry house at Halifax, N. S., lately a few of the valuable little tokens were found under a board where they had slipped while being handled by ferry agents. Parties corresponding with J. H., box 145, can get further particulars.

We understand it is in contemplation to issue a Brant memorial medal this summer, also a medal to commemorate Toronto Musical Festival to be held this summer. Further descriptions will be given at time of issue.

Among a valuable collection of American coins which I purchased lately was the "Tin Continental Currency Dollar." Legend continental currency, date 1776 below. "Mind your business," below the dial; "Fugio" near the sun and under "Continental." These pieces are as large as a silver dollar. On the obv. thirteen rings linked bears the name of a state.

A very handsome medal to commemorate the International Demonstration of Odd Fellows held at Brockville, July, 1884. Obv. in centre, a camp, on each side a guard with spear; above, the all seeing eye; under tent, three links with initials F. H. C., one letter in each link; "Brockville, July, 1884," in raised letters around two-thirds circle. Rev. two flags crossed; Stars and Stripes to left, and Union Jack to right. I. O. O. F., in raised letters between upper portion in semi; the two flags are bound together at bottom by the three links with F. L. T., one letter in centre of each link. Around the upper circle "International," and the lower sweep "Demonstration."

White metal, size 20.

The new twenty-five cent pieces are not as well executed as the other previous dates. The absence of Ralph Heaton's initial H. below the wreath, has led to the impression that they are counterfeit. They are pronounced all right by the authorities.

The 1804 dollar is the rarest piece among the American series. Many of them have been sold for $1,000. The reason of their rarity is that in 1804 was the war with the Barbary pirates. An expedition was sent over from the United States. The expedition staid much longer than was expected, and as money was needed, the whole amount of the 1804 dollars coined was sent there. The sailors who received these dollars gave them to the natives for supplies and for presents for their friends at home. The natives used them as "amulets" or charms, and most of them were carried far into the interior.

Exchanges.

In order to facilitate the exchange of duplicates, and with a view to bringing about more intimate relations among collectors, we offer a column per month, *free of charge to our subscribers only,* wherein they may state what they have to dispose of and what they desire in exchange. Notices must be written on a separate sheet of paper.

Old Canadian and Provincial stamps and coins to exchange for those not in my collection. Some good books for coins or stamps. Send list of what you have. Address, M. A. MacDonald, Eldon, Prince Edward Island.

Will exchange any of the following, viz: all kinds of bill stamps, U. S. Special Delivery stamps on original envelopes, specimens of coal fossils, plants, ferns, etc., for good foreign or old Canadian stamps not in my collection. State what you have. All letters answered by return mail. T. J. McMinn, 102 Rose Avenue, Toronto.

We will give 50 foreign stamps (all different) for every one of the following countries : Chili, Tobago, Cyprus, Dominica or any central American and South American countries. Send list. Gibson Bros., Ingersoll, Ont., Canada.

A woman was sentenced in an English court to six months' hard labor as a rogue and a vagabond, her crime being that she was in the habit of carrying a sealed and addressed envelope in her hand, and soliciting from passers-by a penny to buy a postage stamp.

The Utica *Observer* a few days ago received a returned letter that was sent out from its office over ten years ago. It was directed to "G. C. Gilbert, Esq., care of the United States Consul, Lima, Peru," and where it has been all these years even the many United States and Peruvian postage stamps with which the envelope is decorated fail to tell.

An epistle of a novel character passed through the Portland, Oregon, postoffice. The novelty consisted in the material upon which it was written, which was a gentleman's linen cuff. There was nothing unusual in the contents, which was simply a dun couched in the following language :—" Please call around and pay your wash bill. Your Laundryman." The cuff was adorned with a two-cent stamp.

Correspondence.

We solicit, and are prepared to insert under this heading, any information or suggestions that may be thought of interest to the Philatelic world. Should anyone wish to have any point explained, upon which their mind is not quite clear, we shall be glad to insert the problem in this department, and in the next number will insert the solutions as given by our readers, so that the questions will be fully answered by different parties, and from different standpoints. Those who think they can give any information on any of the subjects inquired about, are cordially invited to give their ideas by writing to the editor of this paper, mentioning the signature to the query, and the communication will be published in the next issue also. We hold ourselves in readiness to give here such information as lies in our power, and are prepared, at all times, to assist Philatelists in the solution of such questions as we are able to.

H. P. (Berlin).—We cannot accept your offer.

Philadelphia.—No. Morell's Philatelic Directory is 25 cents, post free.

E. S. (Galt).—Your stamp is an Austrian receipt stamp.

A Subscriber in New York.—The value of the blue stamp was 1 kreuzer, that of the yellow 10 kr., and that of the rose 50 kr. They served to prepay one, ten, or fifty newspapers at once, and were exclusively for home postage. The large "double-headed eagle" journal stamps were used for foreign postage only.

John Moncrief.—Look in another column and you will find the information you desire.

Subscriber.—The stamp you describe is a Japan not a China.

Collector (Perth).—You can be supplied with volume 1 at this office, price twenty-five cents.

L. B.—Durbin's catalogue will answer, it is not illustrated but it gives a very good description of every stamp.

The year before the introduction of cheap postage into England the average number of letters written by each person in a year was three. The next year it was seven ; it is now thirty-six. In 1839 there were eighty-two million letters posted, of which about one in every thirteen was franked. In 1840 the circulation rose to one hundred and sixty-nine million, although franking was abolished. At the present time it has reached the astonishing total of one thousand two hundred and eighty million.

When answering advertisements kindly mention this paper.

— THE —

Toronto Philatelic Journal.

A MONTHLY MAGAZINE

DEVOTED TO THE INTEREST OF STAMP COLLECTORS.

Price 25 Cents Per Annum.

MAY, 1886.

H. MORELL,

PUBLISHER,

76 Baldwin Street, Toronto, Canada.

THE
Toronto Philatelic Journal.

VOL. II.   TORONTO, MAY, 1886.   No. 3.

Record of New Issues.

Any information our readers can give us at any time, regarding recent emissions or changes, will be gratefully received and credited.

BERMUDA.—The following change in colors is reported : 2 pence, brown-violet ; 6 pence, purple ; 1 shilling, brown.

CYPRUS.—A new value has been issued, viz. : 12 paras, red.

DUTCH EAST INDIES have issued a wrapper stamp, value ten cents. Color will be given next month.

DOMINICA. — The 6d. green has been surcharged "Half Penny " in black.

GUATEMALA.—We herewith present our readers with an illustration of the surcharged stamp mentioned in our last month's journal. These consist of the stock of stamps used for the payment of Northern railway tax.

GUINEA.—A new design is said to have been prepared but has not yet been put in circulation.

HOLKAR.—This Indian state has issued a stamp (see illustration), ½ anna mauve. The stamp measures about 25x30 mm.

ITALY.-Letter cards are in contemplation, of the value of 15 centesimi.

PERSIA.—There is a set of unpaid letter stamps copied after those of France. On an oblique band is " A Percevoir," at the top " Perse " and in lower right hand corner the value in a circle. Talues, 1, 2, 5, 6, 10, 15 shahi, 1, 2, 5 kran, 1 toman, all printed in indigo and perforated 13. The stamps surcharged " official " are as follows : with horizontal surcharge, 6sh. on 5sh. green, 12sh. on 50c. black, 18sh. on 10sh. orange, 1 toman on 5fc. red, with oblique surcharge, 6sh. on 5sh. green. There is no 12sh. on 10c. as previously reported. The 5 kran, violet has appeared same type as the small stamp with head, and the 1 toman yellow brown is expected soon.

PHILIPPINE I.—The 2⅜c. blue is surcharged " Habilitado pa, correos de 16 cts." in carmine.

PORTUGAL. The 25 reis, according *Le Timbre Poste* is red brown.

ROUMANIA. Of the new type, the 5 and 25 bani have been issued.

SERVIA.—A double postal union card, 10 paras, brown on yellow, is said to have been issued.

STRAITS SETTLEMENTS.—Double 1 and 3 cent cards are now in use.

TOBAGO.—A penny postal card has been prepared, carmine on buff.

U. S. OF COLUMBIA. A new 10c. stamp has been issued (see illustration) the portrait is that of Dr. Vanez, president of the republic.

VENEZUELA.—A new edition of cards is reported on various colors, with " Tarjeta Postal " in ornamental shaded letters instead of plain letters.

Written for the Toronto Philatelic Journal.

THE FIRST U.S. ENVELOPES.

BY WILL M. CLEMENS.

The original form of letter postage was the envelope adopted by Great Britain in 1840. Prepaid envelopes became very popular, and were largely used, but not in the form first introduced. Although the postal authorities of the United States moved very slowly in the matter of adopting adhesive stamps, they moved still more slowly in the matter of envelopes. In August, 1853, two years after the first regular issue of stamps were made, the first Government envelopes appeared. Two values were at first employed—the envelope of three cents, and one of six cents. The design, embossed on a plain, colored disk, consists of a profile bust of Washington, after the famous statue by Houden, turned to the left, with an upright, oval frame, enclosing at the top and bottom, labels of the value, (three or six above, cents below.) At either side of the frame, connecting the labels, is a simple, engine-turned pattern, composed of interlacing lines, three and three, forming a series of loops, these loops varying in number, and are the chief means of detecting the several kinds of stamps. The color of the three cent stamp was red, that of the six cent stamp being green. In October of the same year, a large, official envelope was issued bearing the six cents with the color changed to red, and in April, 1855, an additional stamp was issued, a ten cent issue printed in green. These different values, 3, 6 and 10 cent, remained in use from 1853 to 1860, and during these years were subject to many changes, both of the stamp, and also the size and shape of the envelope. It is believed that two dies of the THREE CENTS were prepared. It is a well-known fact that the second die became badly worn, in consequence of the immense amount of work it had to perform. As a result, the ends of the labels, (the parts most likely to wear), were trimmed. These slight alterations have produced four distinct varieties as follows:

DIE ONE.—The ends of the labels are straight, and but seven loops are formed in each label by the intersecting lines. The words, "three" and "cents" occupy much more space than any of the other values. The ends of the labels are much further from the first and last letters of the value.

SECOND DIE.—*Type 1.* The ends of the labels are curved, the first and last letters of the value nearly touch them, and the intersecting lines form ten loops on one side, and nine on the other.

SECOND DIE.—*Type 2.* The ends of the labels are straight, with their angles intersected by portions of the interlaced lines, the loops counting eight and a half by nine.

SECOND DIE—*Type 3.* The ends of the labels are straight, ending in a distinct line.

SECOND DIE.—*Type 4.* The ends of the labels are slightly curved without any lines at the four ends, as in type 3.

SECOND DIE.—*Type 5.* The ends of the labels are curved. This is the most common variety.

The die for the six cent stamp is precisely similar to the type 3, described above. The ten cent has two distinct dies, one similar to the six cent impression, the other like the first of the three cent envelopes. There were three sizes of envelopes used for this series—note, letter and official. The six cent was both letter and official size, the ten cent only letter size, while the three cent was used in note and letter size. There are many other details connected with this first issue of United States Envelope Stamps which the philatelist might well study with learning and profit. They are among the rare stamps of the United States, and some of the varieties I have named, command high and even fabulous prices.

Frederick N. Palmer, the Boston physician who jumped from a Portland steamer last week and was drowned with his four-year-old grandchild, was postmaster at Brattleboro, Vt., during Polk's Administration. He was the originator of the first American postage stamp, which was engraved for the postmaster's personal use. These stamps were in use long before the Government decided to use stamps for the prepayment of postage. The Palmer stamps bring a fabulous price, one having recently sold for $145, while a few years ago one sold for $300 at auction.

A PHILATELIC SCRAP-BOOK.

BY H. A. T.

This idea of a scrap-book may have suggested itself to some of you or you may have read of the idea before.

I read recently in a well known collector's journal, of societies having scrap-books, but no mention of individuals having any was made; this article also mentioned having the books on minerals, birds' eggs, etc., but it said nothing about any on Philately.

Now, I think that, at the present time, Philately is mentioned more than any other collector's hobby, in the daily and weekly papers and in the magazines; and if anything deserves a scrap-book, Philately does.

It is but a very short time ago, that I noticed in a single issue of one of the daily papers, a half-column article and one or two smaller notices devoted entirely to the subject of stamp collecting.

Stamp collectors, if you want to have something interesting and useful pertaining to your hobby, start a scrap-book without delay and you will not regret it.

Now, to begin with, take a useless blank book that you or some of your friends may have, or if you prefer, buy a scrap-book of some bookseller. Then keep a lookout for notes or articles on Philately and when one is found, paste it in your book.

Thus a beginning is made and although this first note or article will not perhaps seem very interesting or desirable, in looking over the book six months or a year afterward it may give you just the information you wished or set your mind at rest on some point on which it was unsettled.

Here there comes up one thing which I wish to speak about, if you should happen to receive a copy of some Philatelic paper, and after reading it, see something that would be good for your scrap book, *do not cut it out* and put it in your book, but preserve the paper carefully as odd numbers of Philatelic papers are nearly always in demand, and one with an article or note cut out would be almost worthless. Get the material for your book from other than Philatelical publications.

Now that you have got your book well under way, keep a lookout for items and before you realize it your book will be full, and when looking it over some future time, you will never regret that you started "A Philatelic Scrap-Book."—*Stamp World.*

The postal route from Claryville to Big Indian, a distance of 21 miles, is through the roughest and wildest portion of the Catskill Mountains. The road is rough, in fact, that the mail is carried on foot, and the carrier is Clark North, who is totally blind. He has carried the United States mail over almost impassable Catskill routes for 30 years, since he was a boy, and has never seen any of the wild region through which he has travelled, and he has never met with an accident; though snow drifts and floods often cross his path yet they seem to be no barrier to him.

At the auction sale of April 12th and 13th, the Brattleboro stamp brought $145; the Goliad, Texas, $95; Baton Rogue, $50; St. Louis, 5c. $55; Newfoundland 1sh. $55; two Hawaii, 1852, 13c. $82 and $90; Canada, 12d. $50; and several others over $50 each.

The Postage Stamps of the World, issued since their first introduction, are estimated at some 6,000. The different kinds bear the heads of five Emperors, eighteen Kings, three Queens, one Grand Duke, six Princes, one Princess, and a number of Presidents, while some bear coats of arms and other emblems, such as the papal keys, &c. There is an admirable collection of stamps in the Berlin Post Office Museum, which last July contained 4,498 specimens—2,462 belonging to Europe, 441 Asia, 251 to Africa, 201 to Australia, and 1,143 to America.

A few days ago a number of Italians went into the Rondout, N. Y., Postoffice and asked for letters. One was handed an epistle, on which was due ten cents postage. A few mornings later the same man handed one of the clerks ten cents and said :—"Tenna centa. Wanta nother lettee."

TORONTO

PHILATELIC JOURNAL

Published on the 15th of every month.

SUBSCRIPTION PRICE.

United States and Canada, 25 cents a year; Foreign
Countries, 35 cents.

ADVERTISING RATES.

Per inch, - - - - - -	$ 50
Per half inch, - - - - -	30
Per column, - - - - -	2 75
Per half column, - - - -	1 50
Per page, - - - - - -	5 00

Twenty per cent. discount given on standing advertisements of over three months.
All advertisements must be in by the 10th of the month
to insure insertion in the same number.

TERMS STRICTLY CASH IN ADVANCE.

Except amounts under $1.00, which may be remitted
in one and two cent stamps.
Address all communications to

H. MORELL,

Editor and Publisher,

76 BALDWIN ST., TORONTO, CANADA.

The Philatelic Journal of America has
"gone into" Philatelic Organization. In the
May number many of the leading philatelists
express their views on the subject, mostly all
in favor, and deservedly.

Now that the summer months are at hand
the philatelic journals will be issuing double
numbers, amalgamating or suspending. We
have already noted the following : *The Foreign Stamp Collectors' News, The Philatelic
Star* and *The Stamp Dealers' Journal* are to
be amalgamated ; *The Philatelic Magazine*
and *Collectors' Companion* have suspended
and *The Exchange,* of Adrian, Mich., has issued its last number.

A certain person, who signs himself "Nagrom," furnished an article entitled "Universal
Postal System" to the *New York Collector* for
their March number and 46 lines of the article, commencing at the third paragraph,
were the composition of Mr. C. E. Swope,
jr., of Louisville, Ky., being part of a treatise
on the Origin and Progress of the Postal Service, written by Mr. Swope and published in
the TORONTO PHILATELIC JOURNAL in May,
1885. "Nagrom" put those 46 lines in the
middle of his little piece so Mr. Swope
wouldn't see them. Mr. Swope did see them
however, and everybody who saw them knows
they were Mr. Swope's work, and now poor
Nagrom is disgraced forever.

His right name is Morgan, but a man who
plagiarizes generally hides his name and often
spells it backward as this one does.—*Plain
Talk.*

THE STAMP AUCTION.

The recent stamp auction held in St.
Louis was a decided success. The attend-
ance was comparatively small, but bids were
executed for several hundred collectors and
dealers who could not attend, through Messrs.
Chas. Votier, of the St. Louis Postage Stamp
Co., and C. H. Mekeel, of the Carson Stamp
Co.

The rarities and choice lots for dealers
brought good prices, as the above named
stamp firms are well known to be the leading
dealers in South and Central American
stamps.

The catalogue did not contain any extremely rare stamps, but a collector in Germany and a member of the Dresden Philatelical Society, purchased $107 worth of
stamps for his collection.

The $200 revenue, catalogued by Sterling
for $25 brought $13. Lot 390, Venezuela
inland postage brought $5 ; and lot 391,
same, next issue, $8.75.

The sale netted over $500, and its success
has secured St. Louis a series of auction
sales, to commence September 15th, and
occur every two months.

Parties desiring to dispose of collections or
specialties are invited to correspond with
either of the above named parties, for terms, etc.

After the sale the reorganization of the St.
Louis Philatelical Society was discussed with
a view of its becoming a chapter of the
National Philatelical Association soon to be
organized. The idea was favored by all
present, and a meeting will be called at an
early date.—*The Carson Philatelist.*

Among Our Exchanges.

We desire to exchange with every paper in the world published in the interest of, or having a department pertaining to Philately.

Publishers, please send us two (2) copies of your paper each month, and we will be pleased to reciprocate.

The Philatelic News is a very neat little paper from Chicago ; it promises to succeed.

The most fashionable, and one of the best stamp papers published, is *The Empire State Philatelist.* Mr. Cuno's "Co-operation" is its special feature for April.

The Capital City Philatelist is one of *the* stamp papers which has worked its way to the top of the ladder. It is well supported by reliable dealers whose advertisements appear each month. With its April number it has started to illustrate the new issues.

The Exchange, of Adrian, Mich., has suspended. We have received number 4 of Volume II., which will be the last number published. It contains a cut of Mr. E. A. Holton, of Boston, Mass., one of the leading stamp dealers in America.

The Minnesota Philatelist will not be published any more as its editor and publisher is at present in the St. Paul (gaol) for making fraudulent use of the U. S. Mails.

All philatelists should read Mr. Bradt's article on " A National Philatelical Organization " in April number of *The Philatelic Journal of America.*

We have also received the following papers. Publishers accept our thanks : *The Philatelic Exchange List, The Stamp and Coin Gazette, Tidings from Nature, The Monthly Call, Collectors' Science Monthly, The Southampton Stamp Advertiser, Stamp and Coin Collector's Advertiser, Carson Philatelist The Observer, Youth's Pilot, Canadian Philatelic and Curio Advertiser, The Philatelic World, Philatelic Tribune, El Ecuador Filatelico, Philatelic Mercury, Quaker City Philatelist, Philatelic Monthly, Welt Post, Arizona Pride of Philately, Youth's Ledger.*

The sale of coins of ancient Greece and Rome war medals and modern coins at New York, April 10th, was a success. Total realized, about $4,000.

STELLALAND.

The Boers of the Transvaal Republic established the republic of Stellaland in 1884. It was on territory claimed by Great Britain, or ground considered necessary for the safety of Natal, and so it was formally "annexed" without many protests on the part of the settlers. As a separate country its existence extended over the space of but a few months. From information which we consider entirely reliable, we are satisfied that the Boer Government issued the postage stamp known to collectors. They had a regularly organized government and being familiar with the advantages of the postal system in their native country, it is not wonderful that they desired the same facilities for the transmission of mail matter in their new home. The fact that the stamps were not available for postage beyond the borders of the country, is nothing against them. There are numerous examples of such stamps, prominent among them being those from Shanghai, which every collector knows of and the genuineness of which no one doubts. If one wants to send a letter from Shanghai to a foreign country, he must prepay with stamps of Japan, France, etc., procured from the different consuls.—*Philatelic Monthly.*

A letter was received the other day at the Oswego Post-office from England addressed to " John Kent, Horse Wiggers Falls, Horse Wiggers County, State of New York." An astute clerk in the Postoffice, after a moment of puzzled thought, decided that the intent of the writer was to have it go to Oswego Falls, Oswego County, and he sent it there.

A lady in Naugatuck, while looking over the old family bible recently, found an old Colonial $6 note, date 1758. The note was good for seventeen ounces, ten pennyweights of silver in New Jersey. On one side is printed, "To counterfeit this is death." The family, evidently, had not followed the injunction, "Search the Scriptures."

The number of ordinary dead letters, circulars and post cards received at the Dead Letter Office, Ottawa, during the year of 1885, was 694,556.

Numismatic Department.

BY J. HOOPER.

All correspondence and information intended for this department should be addressed to J. Hooper, Esq., Box 145, Port Hope, Cana_a.

Our brave volunteers' "North West" medals have arrived and are being distributed among the men who took part in that campaign. They are of silver, size 23. Obverse, coronated head of Queen Victoria with veil thrown over back of head ; around circle the words "Victoria Regina et Imperatrix.". Reverse, "North West" in semi ; "1885 Canada" in two straight lines. The above words are surrounded by a branch of maple leaves, the stem starting at bottom and continuing in one line around outer circle ; under the bust is the name of the maker, "J. G. Wyou." The medal is exceptionally well executed, more especially the obverse which bears a good likeness of "our Queen." The continuous branch of maples will bear criticism to an artist in that line, the double branched wreath would have (perhaps) been more artistic. However, as a whole, the medal is well produced and the letters in good shape. The medal a clasp with red and slate colored striped ribbon. A cast miniature medal is also to hand and will be described in our next, together with the "Egyptian Nile Voyageurs'" medal.

The oldest bank note in existence is preserved in the Museum at St. Petersburg. Its date is 1399 B.C. It was issued by the Chinese Government. Bank notes were current in China 2697 B.C. The note is written and bears the name of the Imperial Bank, date and number of issue, signature of a Mandarin and contains a list of punishments inflicted for forgery of notes.

A coin found near Scituate, Mass., U.S., bears on the obverse the following inscription : "In commemoration of the extinction of Colonial slavery throughout the British dominions in the reign of William IV." The reverse has the figure of a slave with his shackles broken and the words, "This is the Lord's doings, 1784."

TO RESTORE WORN COIN.

While Dr. A. H. Best, of North Carolina, was silver plating a small article with cyanide of silver solution he used a Spanish silver coin as an anode. The coin had been hammered to twice its original size and was worn perfectly smooth. A powerful glass could not bring out a letter or figure on it, yet in a little while after it was put in the bath every letter and figure became perfectly clear. The date, 1800, could be plainly seen.

A singular discovery of gold coins has been made at Park Street, a little village on the Southern borders of Belfordshire, and has been reported to the Treasury. A man in the employment of Mr. Boff, carpenter and builder, was engaged splitting some old oak beams, when in the centre of one of them he came upon a cavity out of which rolled a number of bright coins. The hole had been neatly formed, and was circular in shape, having apparently been drilled into the wood, and it was fitted with a plug to conceal it. On further search being made, another hiding place of the same kind was found, also containing treasure. The coins, which number over a hundred, consist of nobles, angels, and half-angels, and vary in date from the reign of Henry VI. to that of Henry the VIII. They are in excellent preservation. Some of them bear the figure of St. Michael, others a ship with a cross for a mast, and all have Latin inscriptions upon them. The largest coins are about the size of half a crown, and the smallest resemble a sovereign. It is not known at present where the beam in which the treasure was found came from, as Mr. Boff has recently pulled down several oldf arm houses and other buildings in the neighborhood.

London postmen are perhaps too busy to read post cards, or one handed in at the post-office of a theatrical newspaper must have perplexed the deliverer if he was not well posted in theatrical technicalities. It was thus couched:—" Please change my head at top this week. Alter juvenile lead to heavies, and say double-handed cornerinan wanted immediately." The advertisement came from the proprietor of a travelling theatre.

Exchanges.

In order to facilitate the exchange of duplicates, and with a view to bringing about more intimate relations among collectors, we offer a column per month, *free of charge to our subscribers only*, wherein they may state what they have to dispose of and what they desire in exchange. Notices must be written on a separate sheet of paper.

I have 10 V Nickles without the word cents each of which I would like to change for 400 Canadian Stamps. Carl Duncker, 800 Carr St., St. Louis, Mo., U.S.

Wanted to Exchange : A 22 calibre revolver with box of cartridges for the best offer of old Canada, N. F., N. B., P. E. I., etc. Robert L. Stephens, State Line, Warren Co., Ind.

Old Canadian and Provincial stamps and coins to exchange for those not in my collection. Some good books for coins or stamps. Send list of what you have. Address, M. A. MacDonald, Eldon, Prince Edward Island.

Will exchange any of the following, viz. : all kinds of bill stamps, U.S. Special Delivery stamps on original envelopes, specimens of coal fossils, plants, ferns, etc., for good foreign or old Canadian stamps not in my collection. State what you have. All letters answered by return mail T. J. McMinn, 102 Rose Avenue, Toronto.

We will give 50 foreign stamps (all different) for every one of the following countries : Chili, Tobago, Cyprus, Dominica or any Central American and South American countries. Send list. Gibson Bros., Ingersoll, Ont., Canada.

50 Sea Shells for every 25 Official, 100 Revenue or 100 old issue U. S. Stamps. Will M. Clemens, Jamestown, N. Y.

Will exchange all kinds of stamps with advanced collectors. Rare United States stamps especially desired. H. Morell, 76 Baldwin St., Toronto, Can.

6 West India sea beans for every 200 mixed Canadian stamps. Will M. Clemens, Jamestown, N. Y.

Old issue Canadian Stamps Wanted— Pence issue specially desired for cash or exchange. E. Y. Parker, 47 Huron Street, Toronto.

Correspondence.

We solicit, and are prepared to insert under this heading, any information or suggestions that may be thought of interest to the Philatelic world. Should anyone wish to have any point explained, upon which their mind is not quite clear, we shall be glad to insert the problem in this department, and in the next number will insert the solutions as given by our readers, so that the questions will be fully answered by different parties, and from different standpoints. Those who think they can give any information on any of the subjects inquired about, are cordially invited to give their ideas by writing to the editor of this paper, mentioning the signature to the query, and the communication will be published in the next issue also. We hold ourselves in readiness to give here such information as lies in our power, and are prepared, at all times, to assist Philatelists in the solution of such questions as we are able to.

Toronto, 10th May, 1886,

Editor Toronto Philatelic Journal.

Dear Sir, — I have in my collection, the set of three Italy, 1855 issue, head of Victor Emanuel, to right in white oval, inscriptions embossed in color, unperforated, and although these stamps are catalogued as the 1855 issue, one of them, the 40 cent red, bears the postmark Torino, 20 Marz, '54. The others, 5 cent and 10 cent, bear only the cancellation marks. There can be no doubt of their genuineness, and I would like to know whether you or any of your readers can inform me how it is that the date is 20 March 1854, when by the catalogues they were not issued until 1855.

I remain,
Yours respectfully,
T. J. McMinn.

102 Rose Avenue,
Toronto.

R. L. Stephens.—Almost all the large dealers in the U. S. have foreign revenues in stock.

Chas. Raines —No, they are not allowed to be brought into the U. S., do not buy them.

Chicago.—We only insert advertisements for cash. You may send your electros by express, prepaid, they are not mailable matter.

J. C. (Phila.)—We can provide you with Vol. I., unbound, 25c., and bound copies, 75c. post free.

Reader.—Published in 1881 by S. South & Co., Brighton, Eng.

OCTOBER 1887.

Toronto Philatelic Journal

A Monthly Magazine For Stamp Collectors

CANADA
NORTH AMERICA

SOUTH AMERICA

TORONTO PHILATELIC COMPANY,
106 HURON STREET.

TORONTO CANADA.

VOL. 2. NO. 4

In answering Advertisements please mention this paper.

Toronto Philatelic Journal.

| VOL. 2. | TORONTO, OCTOBER, 1887. | No. 4. |

Canadian Philatelic Association.

Owing to strenuous efforts put forth during the past summer, the formation of the C. P. A. has become a thing of reality, and the advent of this society, will undoubtedly make philately boom in the land of the beaver and maple leaf. In looking over the list, instead of finding the Queen City of the West represented by at least two score, there are only a solitary *two*. Surely we should let our friends down by the sea know that we are heart and hand with them in this, the most enlightened and intellectual of pursuits,—"Philately." The following is the official list of members, with their numbers :---

1.—John R. Hooper, 124 Slater St., Ottawa, Can.
2. --Fred J. Grenny, P. O. Department Brantford, Ont.
3.—J. A. Leighton, Box 194, Orangeville, Ont.
4.—H. F. Ketcheson, Box 499, Belleville, Ont.
5.—J. C. Niesser, P. O., Toronto, Ont.
6.—R. F. McRae, 573 St. Urbain St., Montreal, P. Q.
7.—Geo. H. Harrison, 629 Dufferin Ave., London, Ont.
8.—J. H. Todd, Box 26, Brandon, Manitoba.
9.—Ernest F. Wurtele, 93 St. Peter St., Quebec, P. Q.
10.—Henry S. Harte, "The Rectory," Petitcodiac, N. B.
11.—F. E. Book, Niagara Falls South, Ont.
12.—H. A. Simpson. Belleville, Ont.
13.—N. E. Carter, Box 314, Delevan, Wisconsin.
14.—H. E. French, Box 60, Niagara Falls South, Ont.
15.—Chas. E. Willis, Box 140. Petitcodiac, N. B.
16.—A. J. Craig, Box 20, Pictou, N. S.
17.—John R. Findlay, Box 185, Halifax, N. S.
18.—Don. A. King, P. O., Halifax, N. S.
19.—F. O. Creed, 6 Smith St., Halifax, N. S.
20.—Olof Larsen, 40 Lockman Street, Halifax, N. S.
21.—S. DeWolf, Box 219, Halifax, N. S.
22.—H. L. Hart, Box 231, Halifax, N. S.
23.—Theo. Larsen, 40 Lockman Street, Halifax, N. S.
24.—Henry Hechler, 184 Argyle Street, Halifax, N. S.
25.—H. Mathers, Box 573, Halifax, N. S.
26.—Chas. G. Woodworth, Box 3003, Denver, Col.
27.—Williston Brown, P. O. Departm't, Charlottetown, P. E. I.
28.—Frank C. Kaye. Halifax, N. S.
29.—J. M. Sheridan, 22 St. Felix Street, Brooklyn, N. Y.
30 —E. F. Smith, 89 Spring Garden Rd., Halifax, N. S.
31.—J. A. Caron, Ste. Luce Station, Rimouski Co., Que.
32.—J. J. Palma, Jr., 124 East 14th St., New York.
33.—George A. Lowe, 106 Huron St., Toronto. Ont.
34.—Edmund A. Smith, 58 Robie St., Halifax, N. S.
35.—A. Lohmeyer, 933 Milton Place, Baltimore, Md.
36.—P. F. O'Keefe, Mansfield Valley, Pa.,
37.—Wilson Willey, 106 Yorkville Ave., Toronto, Ont.

In the above list there are included

lawyers, doctors, government officials, ministers, professional gentlemen, military officers and aldermen. This is a splendid showing, and the above list includes mostly advanced philatelists who have helped to make stamp collecting a science.

It is to be hoped that all good phila- telists will send in their names to the Secretary *pro tem*, Jno. R. Hooper, Ottawa, who is registering those who wish to be- come members. The fee is only 25c. and the annual dues will be settled by a vote when the election of officers takes place.

Two or three names have already been mentioned for the presidency, among whom are Major Hechler, of Halifax, and Mr. Ketcheson, of Belleville. Both are gen- tlemen of ability. and well-qualified. Vice-presidents will be elected for each province, who will superintend the work to be done in their jurisdiction.

Representatives are wanted in British Columbia and the North-West Territories.

The Secretary spent his vacation in corresponding *re* the C. P. A. He reports several applications on hand.

Written for the T. P. J.

Some Valuable Collections.

BY SULLEXAS.

Paris can boast of the largest collections in the world. The collections of Herr Von Ferrary is generally admitted to be the largert and most valuable.

It is said to be worth over $300,000.

The following are among his rarest stamps:

British Guiana, 1856, 4c., worth about $200.

Mauritius one penny and two penny first issue worth about $1,000 the pair, the rare mauritius envelope worth about $200, and a pair of Reunion's worth about $300.

A portion this collection belonged to Mr. Philbrick for which he paid $40,000 and a portion to Sir Danial Cooper to whom he paid the sum of $20,000. .

After Herr Von Ferrary's collection

they are generally admitted to rank as follows:

Mr. T. K. Tappling's M. P., second ; M. M. Caillebotte's, Paris, third ; Baron A de Rothschild's, Paris, fourth ; Dr. Legrand's, Paris, fifth ; M Donati's, Paris, sixth : Mr. J. K. Tiffany's, St. Louis, seventh.

The Continental, Colonial, & British Post Offices.

To the Editor of the T. P. J.

Sir,—Having for some months had my attention directed to the shortcomings of the British Post Offices, as compared with the same department elsewhere, allow me to give your readers some of the results of the information I have received from nearly every country in Europe and in America in reply to questions addressed to their postmasters. I give the results as to various forms of mail matter.

1. Post Cards: We took them from Germany, and adopted a halfpenny post for letters on cards. We were soon after deprived of it, and made to pay $16\frac{1}{4}$ per cent more than a halfpenny for the use of a small piece of rather thick paper. For the poor man who buys a single card even this concession does not exist ; he must pay really a penny, farthings being rare. The department adds 600 per cent for a woodcut on a piece of wood pulp. No other country in Europe or America charges a fraction for the card itself, and Italians can buy a duplicate for a reply, or two cards, at the price of card and a half. The card we give the public is, besides, the smallest in the civilisd world. Italy and Greece give a quarter more, Sweden, France and Turkey nearly a half, and Roumania gives almost twice the size. It is also a fact which free traders cannot find fault with, though English paper makers may, that the Post Offices buys the card itself on the Continent and pays $2\frac{1}{2}$d. to 3d. per ℔ for it, charging 1s. 6d. per ℔ for the printing.

2. Sample Post : We had this at a quarter of the then letter postage, taking

the weight into account, until 1870, and then, as regards the British trader in his own country, it was withdrawn. Anything pulped, whether sheathing, press board, paper for rollers and roofs and walls, is charged now two ounces for ½d., but samples or patterns of anything that will make these things, or anything else, pay letter rates. A great firm sent a quarter of a million of 2oz. samples to France the other day to be posted to English dealers for 1d. each, and saved ½d. each. Foreigners may send by pattern post to England, but not Englishmen to Englishmen.

3. Newspapers: Every four paged paper all over the Continent goes for about the fifth of a penny; every small circular or printed notice for the tenth of a penny in some counties, in others for one-fifth of a penny. Every Canadian paper or periodical is franked to subscribers anywhere in Canada or in the United States, or to newsagents, free; papers or periodicals, between man and man. go at half the British rate, and in New South Wales, where 25½ papers per head go by post, in Queenland, West Australia, Tasmania and Trinidad also. In Malta newspapers are also free and printed matter generally is carried ½lb for ½d.

4. Small Parcel Post: A halfpenny for 4oz. conveys all over the Dominion seeds, roots, cuttings, scions, grafts and bulbs. *Bona fide* samples of anything besides go at the same. Newspapers in the United States are carried free to subscribers in the same county as that of publication, an area of about 1,000 square miles, from post office to post office. If delivered by post carrier, a cent is charged in addition. If sent beyond a county, a cent a copy. But by a certain easy plan they can go in bulk through the post office, 500 for 5s. or ½d. of a penny each. There is also a universal inland sample post at a uniform rate of ½d. for one ounce. Transient or casual newspapers are a ½d. each. Printed matter and books at British rates.

5. Letters: By the world's post offices these are variously charged. In most there is an equivalent to penny postage, but in Canada it is 1½d., Italy and France 2d. In Belgium a folded card of liberal size is sold for one centime, which an adhesive stamp makes private, and which can take the place of sheet and envelope. In nearly all European states, cards announcing births, deaths and marriages, and Chrirtmas, Easter, and New Year exchanges, with names of senders, go in an envelope with an unsealed flap at less than ½d. each. In Belgium travellers advices are one centime in envelopes with unsealed flaps or on cards, and the post carrier, at the wish of the sender, will deliver sealed a bill with a certain form, and the post-office will, if the debtor wishes, take the money and give a receipt.

6. The field of free matter in colonial and American offices is large. In England the only free matter is a parliamentary petition not over 2lb. In Canada no postage is charged on any blue books or reports, or any other matter emanating from or going to the Legislature in any province, or on books for or from the parliamentary libraries, and all documents connected with deaths, births, or marriages (census reports), and those on agriculture, and letters to members of Parliament on parliamentary business are free also. In the United States it is very nearly the same, and greenbacks, or National Bank notes, can in seperate parcels be sent, if not free, at ½d. per ounce all over the Union.

There are many other interesting details of the foreign and colonial offices on which your space forbids me to enter.—

Yours &c., J. H. R.

The carrier pigeon is still a matter of great importance in Paris, where these interesting birds have come into a system of organisation. second only to a postal service. The last siege was an occasion when these birds did incalculable service, when all other means of communication had been cut off.

TORONTO
ᑭHILATELIC JOURNAL.

Published on the 1st of every month.

Geo. A. Lowe,   **Jos . Hooper,**
ED. PHILATELIC DEPT.   **ED. NUMISMATIC DEPT**

SUBSCRIPTION :

United States and Canada 25c. per year; Foreign Counties'
35c. per year.

Advertising Rates :

1 inch	0 50
2 "	0 80
½ column	1 50
1 "	2 50
1 page	4 50

10 per cent. discount on standing advts.
Copy wanted not later than the 25th.

Remit money by P.O. order, or small amounts in one or
two cent stamps.
Address all correspondence to the

Toronto Philatelic Co.

106 Huron St.   **Toronto, Canada.**

TORONTO, OCTOBER, 1887.

The Journal still lives. After a lapse of a few months, we again make our appearance.

The TORONTO PHILATELIC JOURNAL proved to be the greatest success of any stamp magazine ever published in Canada. It was organized March, 1885, and suspended June, 1886, owing to the publisher not having sufficient time to devote to it.

We have now established the journal on a firm basis. and with the strong band of contributers we have secured, it is bound to rank with the leading philatelic journals.

We had the pleasure of meeting Mr. H. E. French, the Niagara Falls stamp dealer last week. Mr. French was in Toronto to complete arrangements for the publication of the *Canadian Philatelist*.

Forgeries.

On the establishment of the postal system, a system now exciting the admiration of the civilized world, whose denizens have testified their approval in that sincerest form of flattery—imatition, and before the issue of stamps had become an established fact, the greatest possible care was taken to prevent their forgery in any shape or form. For instance, the ground-work of the adhesive stamp was a marvel of fineness obtained by means of engine-turning. It defied competition, and could not be done by hand, and the design could only be seen to advantage by the aid of a powerful magnifying glass; while the threads of coloured silk introduced through the sheets intended to be made into envelopes and covers was of a material entirely beyond the reach of a common counterfeiter. As regards the labels, it was contended that forgery was in itself impracticable, because no forger could have the command of very powerful, delicate, and therefore costly machinery, requiring for its management skilful, and highly-paid workmen. If the Queen's head had alone constituted the effigy, something in imitation might have been done by the aid of lithography, or some other such copying process; but this would have failed when applied to the extremely delicate lines already mentioned as constituting the background. Then the introduction of silk threads into the paper, it being woven in the pulp, made it difficult to manufacture, and very expensive, and with the vigilance of the Excise, forgery was rendered next to impossible.

As a result of these precautionary measures, it has been left on record that "only two attempts at forgery have been made, both of a very bungling character, though in one the author was cunning enough to escape personal detection. In the other which occurred in Ireland, the offender was convicted and punished; the detection occured through the fact that a young man had written to his sweetheart under one of the forged stamps, and enclosed another for her to use in reply." Since the substantial line-engraving gave place to the current type-set adhesives, the contrivances for the detection of fraud, on which the authorities of 1840 plumed themselves, have been swept away.

There is only one imitation of the Mulready known to have passed the post. It has the date "London, 9 My 77" obliterated with the modern circular postmark is an almost sure means of detection, because, at the date of its circulation, all genuine specimens were cancelled with an ornamental Maltese cross struck in red sealing-wax. I have advisedly said "almost" for it should be borne in mind that these, as well as any other obsolete British stamp, are all quite capable of franking letters through the Post down to the present day. But there happily exist many salient points of difference between this forgery and the "true blue," or rather "true black," for no forgery of the twopence—which is the blue—is known. The genuine being printed from a brass plate in *tailledouce*, stands out from the paper in relief, while the copy is simply typographed and presents quite a smooth surface. Between the two designs there is no perceptible unlikeness, but a close inspection and comparision of the copies betrayed the absence of a stop after the engraver's name, and a similar error is found in the letters R. A. appended to that of the artist. The large transverse oval is conspicious by its absence, as are also the silk threads in the paper; and the design being printed on a modern gummed envelope, this should of itself be sufficient to warn everyone of its spurious character.

In a competition among stamp connoisseurs a prize was awarded to a gentleman for producing an exquisite copy of the design found on genuine specimens. So skilfully did the successful competitor accomplish his task that in design, colour, even the tint of the very paper on which the drawing stood, the copy was a pre-

sentment of the original. Being folded as the envelope, with blue edging lines, and showing, in addition, what one would have thought almost impossible of achievement by pen or ink, the word POSTAGE worked on apparently engine-turned ground, exactly as seen in veritable blue Mulreadies, it would have been as much matter for surprise if, on presentation at the Post office, its nature had been detected, as if it had passed unchallenged. In conclusion, to show the nicety attainable by carefully designed pen-and-ink sketches, I will relate a curious case of forging a postage stamp lately reported from Odessa.

An engineer of that town advertised for a draughtsman, requesting all competitors to send in with their application a sample drawing. Both were to be forwarded by post, as no personal interview would be granted. Amongst the letters was one which, on being opened, did not contain any drawing, but called particular attention to the postage stamp on the envelope, which on examination turned out to be a very clever imitation of the seven kopeck postage stamp, drawn by hand with a crow quill and colours. Unfortunately the talented executant did not enjoy any benefits from his skill and ingenuity, for one of the unsuccessful competitors, with more spite than sense, denounced the affair to the authorities, with the result that the young artist was tried and punished for forging a public document with a view of defrauding the Russian revenue of seven kopecks.—*T. M. Wears.*

A carat of gold receives its name from the carat seed, or seed of the Abyssinian coral flower. This was at one period made useful when gems or gold were to be weighed, and so came about the peculiar and now general use of the word. Twenty-two carats fine means that out of twenty-four parts twenty-two are gold and all the rest alloy.

NUMISMATIC DEPARTMENT.

All correspondence in this department should be addressed to Mr. Hooper.

A Coin is in itself a history. There was once a lost city which owes its place to a coin.

For over a thousand years no one knew where Pandosia was. History told us that at Pandosia, King Pyrrhus collected those forces with which he overran Italy, and that he established a mint there; but no one could put their finger on Pandosia.

Eight years ago a coin came under the sharp eyes of a numismatist. There were the letters Pandosia inscribed on it : but, what was better, there was an emblem indicative of a well known river, the Crathis.

Then everything was revealed with the same certainty as if the piece of money had been an atlas, and Pandosia, the mythical city, was at once given its proper position in Bruttium. Now, a coin may be valuable for artistic merit, but when it elucidates a doubtful point in history or geography, its worth is very much enchanced.

This silver coin, which did not weigh more than a shilling, because it cleared up the mystery of Pandosia, was worth to the British Museum £200, the price they paid for it.

The "1838 Bank of Montreal Penny Token," (side view,) in uncirculated condition, realised $30 at W. Ellot Woodwards sale in New York, Aug. 18th last.

The Jubilee Coinage of Her Majesty Queen Victoria appears to give universal dissatisfaction, the work is poorly executed. It is expected that it will not pass into circulation, and as the dies appear to be the same for the silver and gold series, and no denomination inserted to designate value, this would give a great opportunity for gilded frauds. The present Jubilee Coinage will become a rarity, already fancy figures are being asked and paid. The Government will no doubt issue another, and more creditably executed series of coins to perpetuate the 50th anniversary of our beloved Queen's reign.

The 1887 Dominion Cent is to hand, and is of the same type and pattern as the previous years. We should like to see a creditable Jubilee issue for the Dominion and await anxiously its appearance.

Robert McLachlan, Esq., Montreal, is busy preparing the manuscript for a supplementary issue to his recent work. We are promised 450 new and old features. This will include some 120 communion tokens. A feature which Mr. McLachlan has taken up and is being followed by others. Canadian numismatists will be laid under a debt of gratitude to the author for his very able work and aids in this line.

Dr. Leroux also promises shortly an Illustrated Supplement with an extensive series of new features and corrections, we would like to see the Dr.'s corrections of his Sou series, as this has been a brain splitter to many a numismatist, somewhere from 50 to 65 varieties are claimed of these interesting pieces. The issue of the Dr.'s first book cost him some 600 dollars, he states that it has paid all expenses in the sale it has had.

There appears to be quite a difference of opinion, among even advanced Numismatists as to what shall be recognized and admitted into their cabinets. —In *Canadian Coins, Medals* and *Tokens.*

F. J. Joseph, recognizes only government issues.

R. W. McLachlan, any piece of Canadian origin ; but must be struck from Dies with raised letters, etc., whilst

A. J. Boucher, F. R. Campeau, J. Hooper and F. J. Grenny, recognize any metallic piece, that has been used as an advertisement, or medium of exchange, or check in the past or present, even if the insciption is done with a sunken punch. However we leave each to follow his own idea in this line, but cannot see why such tokens (as Cast) by " Oshawa Knights of Labor." (*Iron*),. The Griggs House, London, Ont., " Jewett House, Lindsay," etc., ete., should not be accepted.

Mr. A. W. Franks has presented to the British Museum a most remarkable coin, lately received from India. It is a decadrachm of the Bactrian series, the first ever met with, and bears on the obverse a horseman charging with his lance an elephant, on whose back are two warriors; and on the reverse, a king or zeus standing, holding a thunderbolt and a spear: in the field is a monogram composed of the letters A B. The obverse records some victory of the Greeks over the barbarians, and the reverse may be a representation of Alexander the Great. The coin evidently comes from the district of the Oxus, and was struck about the middle of the second century B.C.

New Medals.

Messrs. P. W. Ellis & Co., Toronto, Ont., have issued two new medals for the Dominion and Industrial Exhibition, Toronto.

The largest size 40 millimetres.

Obverse : Exhibition Main Building with wreath of Maple Leaves on outer circle.

Reverse : British and Canadian Coats of Arms on three district shields surmounted by a sheaf of wheat, oak and maple leaves intertwined, and on the outer circle, the words, "Dominion and Industrial Ehibition, Toronto, 1887."

A description of the smaller medals will follow. These medals are issued in gold, silver and bronze by the firm for the Association, and are intended to be given with the prizes awarded. The Numismatists of Ontario justly feel pride in the excellence and beauty of the various medals this firm has contributed to their collection of " The Medals of Ontario." The work showing evidences of a superior workmanship and execution.

Rare U.S. Dollars and their Value.

1794.—$35 ; 1798, with small eagle, $2 ; 1799, five stars facing, $2 ; 1804—$8 ; 1836 — $5 ; 1838—$25 ; 1839—$15 ; 1851—$20; 1852—$25 ; 1854—$6 ; 1855—$5 ; 1856— $2 ; 1858—$20.

RARE HALF-DOLLARS.

1794—$5 ; 1796—$40 ; 1797—$30 ; 1801 $2 ; 1802—$2 ; 1815—$4 ; 1836, "reeded," $3 ; 1838, "Orleans," $5 ; 1852—$3 ; 1853 "no arrows" $15.

RARE QUARTER-DOLLARS.

1796—$3 ; 1804—$3 ; 1823—$50 ; 1853 "no arrows" $4.

RARE 20C. PIECES.

1874 proof $10 ; 1877 proof $2 ; 1878 proof $2.

RARE 10C. PIECES.

1796—$3 ; 1797, "16 stars," $4 ; 1797 "13 stars" $4.50; 1798— $2 ; 1800— $4 ; 1801 to 1804 each $3 ; 1804—$5 ; 1805 to 1811—50c.; 1811—75c.; 1822— $3 ; 1846—$1.

RARE 5C. PIECES.

1794—$3 ; 1795-75c.; 1796—$2 ; 1797— $2 ; 1800—75 ; 1801—$1.50 ; 1802—50. ; 1803—$1.50 ; 1805—$3 ; 1846—$1.

RARE 3C. PIECES.

1851 to 1855—15c.; 1855—25c.; 1856 to 1862—15c.; 1863 to 1873—50c.

RARE U. S. CENTS.

1793 "with wreath" $2.50 : 1793 "with chain" $3.50; 1793 "with liberty cap" $4 ; 1799—$25 ; 1804 has sold at $200 ; 1809—$1.

RARE HALF CENTS.

1793—$1 ; 1796—$10 ; 1831, 1836, 1840 to 1849 and 1852—$4.

It is said there are only seven genuine 1804 dollars in this country. 1801 issues have been changed by counterfeiters to 1804 so as to almost defy detection.

Exhibition Medals.

Gold and silver medals prepared and struck by Messrs. P. W. Ellis & Co., Toronto, for the Toronto Exhibition of 1887 :

Obverse : Side view busts of the Marquis and Marchioness of Lansdowne, surrounded by wreaths of maple.

Reverse : Two shields on outer belts, " Dominion of Canada," " Industry, Intelligence, Integrity ;" " 1837," " 1887." Underneath, a sheaf of wheat, etc., surmounted by a crown. Intertwined a wreath of Roses, Shamrocks, Thistles, and Maple leaves; on outer circle, " Dominion and Industrial Exhibition, Toronto, 1887." This is one of the best medals issued by this firm so far and bears evidence of a superior workmanship in its execution.

Money.

Of very ancient origin is money. It is mentioned as a medium of commerce in the Bible, in Genesis xxiii, where Abraham purchased a field as a sepulchre for Sarah, in the year of the world 2139. Homer speaks of brass money as existing 1184 B. C. The invention of coin is ascribed to the Lydians. Their money consisted of gold and silver. Iron money was used in Sparta, and iron and tin in Great Britain. Julius Cæsar was the first person who obtained the express permission of the Senate to place his image on the Roman coins. Earlier they had placed the image of their deities on the coins. The Romans called their silver *moneta*, because it was coined in the temple of Juno Moneto, 269 B. C. Money has been made of different materials, even of leather. It was made of pasteboard by the Hollanders as late as 1574. The North American Indians in early times used shells strung together, which they called wampum. Coins were made in many different shapes. English coins were partly square, oblong and round, until the Middle Ages, since when round coins have only been used. The Chinese and Japanese coins are round with a square hole through the cenrre. The names of many obsolete pieces are met with in Shakespeare and some other English authors, such as the angel, angelot, groat, guinea, etc. The first silver coin struck in England was the ancient silver penny. It was struck with a cross so deeply indented that it might be easily parted into two for half-pence and four for farthings.

Collecting Stamps.

The collection of old or used postage stamps is usually encouraged in the young as affording harmless amusement, with the collateral advantage of tending to excite an interest in the study of political geography and contemporary history. The intrinsic value of these curiosities is so trivial that few persons were, at first prepared to find that their acquisition could become an absorbing passion. Yet there is not a civilised country where the mania has not infected a more or less numerous class of enthusiasts. The prices offered in France, for instance, for some of the rarer specimens of *timbres-poste* are extraordinary—reminding us of the sums once lavished by Dutchmen on a rare bulb, or given, in the present day; by Englishmen for a choice orchid. Thus, an old Tuscan stamp of any year prior to 1860 is now fetching £5 in Paris. A sovereign is offered for any French stamp of the year 1849. But these are trifles. A stamp of British Guiana for 1835 will readily fetch from 500 to 1,000 francs; while no less than 2,000 francs (£80) will be paid for an 1847 stamp of another British colony— the Isle of Mauritius. In Paris there are upwards of 150 wholesale Dealers, and the Collectors are numbered by tens of thousands.—*Stamp Collectors' Journal.*

NOVEMBER 1887.

Toronto
Philatelic Journal

A Monthly Magazine
For Stamp Collectors

NORTH
AMERICA

SOUTH
AMERICA

TORONTO PHILATELIC COMPANY,
106 HURON STREET.

TORONTO CANADA.

VOL. 2. NO. 5.

In answering Advertisements please mention this paper.

Toronto Philatelic Journal.

| VOL. 2. | TORONTO, NOVEMBER, 1887. | No. 5. |

Canadian Philatelic Nomination.

The Canadian Philatelic Association is preparing actively for their first election of officers, and nominations are now being received by the secretary. All those who wish to nominate a member must first get that member's permission. This will check indiscriminate nomination, and prevent after trouble in nominees retiring. The offices to be elective are as follows:— President, a Vice-President for each province, Secretary, Treasurer, Exchange Superintendent, Librarian, Official Organ, Counterfeit Detector, an Executive Board of three, and Official Editor. The Purchasing Agent and other minor offices will be elected by the Executive. All elected officers being ex-officio members of the latter. Printed blank forms for voting will be prepared by Mr. Hooper and forwarded after the nominations closes on the 15th November. All nominations should be sent in before November 10th to allow a list to be prepared.

It is with feelings of mixed pride and pleasure that the C. P. A. should start with 60 good and true members. This augurs well for the future, and Mr. Hooper states he confidently expects at least a hundred before the close of the year. All collectors should send in their fees (25c.) at once in order to have a vote at the coming election. There are still a number of live philatelists who have not enrolled their names, but we hope that they will come forward, and above all work harmoniously together for the advancement of "Philately." The secretary *pro-tem.* reports that he has still over 40 applications on hand, and in his canvass for members, he says that if there is one that does not like the new C. P. A. they have very wisely said nothing disparaging to our National Society. *Non nobis solum.* Let the Toronto philatelists fill up the roll-book and become charter members before the election.

The following names have been enrolled since we last went to press.—

38.—H. C. Beardsley. 422 N. 7th Street. St. Joseph, Mo.

39.—H. E. Deats, Flemington, N. J.

40.—E. W. Voute, 307 Webster Avenue, Chicago.

41.—Rudolf Wolilfatirt, Erfurt, Germany.

42.—P. M. Wolsieffer. 162 State Street, Chicago.

43.—W. S. McLean, Neils Harbor, N.S.

44.—C. W. Price, Plymouth, Michigan.

45.—W. D. Boyd, Box 184, Simcoe, Ont.

46.—A E. Warren, Box 1981, Montreal.

47.—S. B. Bradt, 225 Dearborn Street, Chicago.

48.—C. R Gadsden, Grand Crossing, Ill.

49.—W. F. Dent, 192 S. Division Street, Buffalo, N.Y.

50.—G. A. Haskell, 3756 Johnson Place, Chicago.

51.—Dudley Holmes, Goderich, Ont.

52.—A. Liebetrau, Gablonz, Bohemia.

53.—R. A. Baldwin Hart. 768 Sherbrook Street, Montreal.

54.—J. R. Davidson. Brandon, Manitoba.

55.—Karl C. Miner, Hoosick Falls. N.Y.

56.—H. R. Ledyard. 108 Bloor Street W., Toronto.

57.—F. Burnett, Brantford, Ont.

58.—Geo. Walker, Peterborough, Ont.

59.—J. Willis Caldwell, 136 Spring Garden Road, Halifax.

60.—W. E. Simpson, Guysboro', N.S.

61.—A. M. Jones, Hoosick Falls, N.Y.

62—H. C. Kendall. Emmetsburg, Iowa.

63—Chas. W. Pengh. Kossuthg, Indiana

Philatelic Societies and their Use.

BY THEODORE SIDDALL.

There have been a number of articles written, lately, giving advice as to the formation of philatelic societies. These societies, for the first few months while the novelty lasts, are of some benefit to their members.; but after that time interest in them is loosened and their meetings drag along like a horse-car going up hill; and the members, finding nothing to interest them there, stay away, and then the society goes to the bow-wows.

There is not so very much to say about philately after all. There is a great deal of "blowing" done, arguing for and against, but very little new matter is brought up, and what is old is talked dry. Those who argue that philately is a science ought to bring out a fact or so occasionally. In the older sciences there is always something new going on, or news to talk about. Again, they argue that philately teaches history, geography, languages, etc., etc., but in papers edited by the upholders of the "science" howl, we do not find that they put into practice their pet doctrines —no historical items, except perhaps that perennial chesnut about the inventor of postage stamps, or the first postal service.

I think the aim of philatelic societies and philatelic papers ought to be to instruct and interest those who now collect stamps, as well as to induce outsiders to take up the hobby. The meetings of societies could be made very interesting by discussions upon living topics, or contemporary history, without having too much "stamp" in it—for all who ever tried will agree with me when I say it is decidedly a dry job to be forever licking stamps. Societies could in many ways be more attractive to outsiders, who, when they see the charm of collecting stamps, would take it up and make good and useful members of the society, and at the same time still further spread stamp collecting—which last is, or should be, the object of all right minded philatelists.

This is not a merely theoritcal article but is written by one who knows something about the needs of philatelic societies. Some may object to this introduction of outside subjects as tending to draw off interest from stamp collecting, and also as being out of place in a stamp society—in answer to which I would say, that if they cannot make their meetings interesting with stamps alone, and want to keep their society alive, they will suffer a disappointment. As I said above, there is little to be said about stamps, and it has been nearly all said, and about the best way to do it is for a number of collectors to get up a society having an aim, or joint object, of promoting stamp collecting, then make meetings interesting to outsiders, and they will most likely follow the example of the collectors who should be in the majority, and take up the collection of stamps.—*Canadian Philatelist.*

Current Opinion.

From Stamp Collector's Journal.

About ten years ago, the stamp mania proper showed signs of waning. Since then stamp collecting has been somewhat dormant; enthusiasts and numerous Philatelic Societies have gone on steadily, but the gigantic craze, which seized hold of boys in every part of the world, which gave rise to Stamp Collecting Journals without number, and sent the prices of very ordinary specimens to a premium, has vanished. Of the merits of stamp collecting as a pursuit, it would be somewhat difficult to speak. Yet, when we consider that men learned in law, Members of Parliament, financiers, diplomatists, and eminent literary men have adopted the pastime, it must be confessed that there is more in it than seen by the unphilatelic eye. The extent of the stamp collecting world is not generally know. There is a Society, meeting at certain intervals in the rooms of one of the best known of Her Majesty's Q C's, which has it correspondents in every civilised land.

New Issues.

From Philatelic Gazette.

AZORES.—The new cards and stamps of 20 reis have been surcharged in small letters.

BULGARIA—*Le Timbre Poste* chronicles the 20s. pale blue and 50s. green.

BR. BECHUANALAND—The Patent stamps of Great Britain, 1872, with "British—Bechuanaland— Postage and Revenue' have been surcharged in three lines in black in place of the word "Patent." We have seen the 1d., 3d., and 6d. lilac, on paper watermarked with "orb" thus surcharged, and the 1s. on paper watermarked "V.R."

BR. LEVANT—The 5 pence of the new type has been issued with the surcharge 80 paras in black.

COCHIN CHINA—The *Timbre Poste* reports a variety of the 25c., black on pink, with triple surcharge, twice with the small figure "5" and "C CH" and once with the large figure "5" This stamp has previously been reported with the double surcharge of the figure "5."

CEYLON—There is a 5c envelope, same type as the 4c. Blue on white paper, 140 x 78mm. The "Ill. Briefmarken Journal" reports the 6c. post-card as being surcharged "2½ cents" in black over the value.

DENMARK—The inscription on the cards will be changed slightly. The 10 ore Postal Union card has been issued with the inscription *verden-post/oreningen (union postale universelle)—Denmark—breckort (carte postale)* in four lines, the top one arched.

FRANCE—The 15c. letter card has been surcharged " Vendue 5 centimes."

MACAO—The 100 reis is surcharged " 5—Reis", and the 200 reis " 10—Reis," each in two lines. The 80 reis is found with and without accent over the final "e."

MAURITIUS—At Port Louis the 13c. grey, surcharged " 2 cents " in red was on sale four hours, July 6th, pending the arrival of a supply of 2c. stamps. Only 40 of the 2400 surcharged, were sold for use, the balance being sold in equal quantities to 13 dealers who hope to make a fortune out of them.

UNITED STATES—The 2c. stamp is now green, 3c. vermilion, 4c. carmine, 5c. blue head of Grant) 30c. brown, 90c. purple, and the envelopes have been changed in color to correspond. The 1c., 2c., 4c. and 5c. are of new types, the latter having head of Grant. A new letter sheet (2c,) has been issued with "Series I" in the upper left hand corner and with watermark "U S" in monogram.

VICTORIA.—The 4c. registry envelope, pink, has now the words "Stamp Duty."

C. P. A.

OUR TICKET.

FOR PRESIDENT.

Henry Hechler, Halifax.

FOR VICE-PRESIDENT.

Ontario—H. F. Ketcheson, Belleville.

Nova Scotia—S. DeWolf, Halifax.

Quebec—Ernest F. Wurtele, Quebec.

New Brunswick—Henry S. Harte. Petit-codiac.

Prince Edward Island--Williston Brown. Charlottetown.

Manitoba—J. H. Todd, Brandon.

FOR TREASURER.

T. J. McMinn, Toronto (formerly Treasurer Toronto Philatelic Society.

EXCHANGE SUPERINTENDENT.

Fred. J. Grenny, Brantford.

EXECUTIVE COMMITTEE.

R. F. McRae, Theo. Larsen and A. E. Warren.

FOR OFFICIAL ORGAN.

TORONTO PHILATELIC JOURNAL.

OFFICIAL EDITOR.

E. Y. Parker, Toronto.

LIBRARIAN.

Rev. Mr. Barnes, Montreal.

TORONTO
₱HILATELIG ꞋOUꞋNAL.

Published on the 1st of every month.

Geo. A. Lowe,   **Jos . Hooper,**
ED. PHILATELIC DEPT.   ED. NUMISMATIC DEPT

SUBSCRIPTION :

United States and Canada 25c. per year; Foreign Counties,
35c. per year.

Advertising Rates :

1 inch...	0 50
2 "	0 80
½ column	1 50
1 "	2 50
1 page...	4 50

10 per cent. discount on standing advts.
Copy wanted not later than the 25th.

Remit money by P.O. order, or small amounts in one or
two cent stamps.
Address all correspondence to the

Toronto Philatelic Co.

106 Huron St.   **Toronto, Canada.**

TORONTO, NOVEMBER, 1887.

THE OFFICIAL CALL.

C.P.A. nominations are now open and
our list published elsewhere shows, that
there is good material to choose the officers
from.   Members will forward their nominations before the 10th November to Mr.
Hooper, the secretary *pro tem.* at Ottawa.
As soon as the nominations close, printed
forms and ballot papers will be sent out to
all members, which will be marked and
returned immediately to the secretary.
All members will receive a copy of this
paper, and should carefully preserve the
lists of members which is complete up to
date.   Whether elected to an office or not,
let all unite to work for the interests of
the Association. . The Exchange Department will be run on similar lines to the
A.P.A.   The duties of all the offices

require hard work, and there should not
be one nominated, who does not consent
to discharge the duties incumbent upon
him to the best of his ability.

We publish elsewhere a ticket which
several members have submitted for the
forth-coming election of the Canadian
Philatelic Association.

We beg to offer the TORONTO PHILA-
TELIC JOURNAL as a candidate for official
organ.

The January number of the Journal will
be increasd to double its present size
and will compete with any philatelic
magazine published in America.

All members of the Association will
receive copies each month gratis.

Messrs. Sheridan, Price, Dent and two
or three other American members of the
C.P.A. are old Canadian boys.

C. P. A.

Just as we go to press we have received the following additional list of
members :—

64 — Dr. E. E. Book, Niagara Falls South,
    Ont.
65.—Rev. Wm. S. Barnes, 118 Union
    Avenue, Montreal.
66.—T. J. McMinn, 102 Rose Avenue,
    Toronto.
67.—Ed. F. Parker, 47 Huron Street,
    Toronto.
68.—J. E. Gass, 208 Argyle Street, Hali-
    fax, N.S.

Increase your Canadian trade by advertising in the TORONTO PHILATELIC
JOURNAL.

NUMISMATIC DEPARTMENT.

All correspondence in this department should be addressed to Mr. Jos. Hooper, Box 145, Port Hope.

THE Prize Medal struck by Messrs. Ellis & Co. for the P. ris, Ont., Exhibition is described as follows: Obverse—Stallion, surrounded by Maple Wreath and corded outer circle. Reverse: Wreath, composed of wheat heads with plain centre to receive recipient's name. Size, 24 M. The obverse of above medal was engraved and first used in 1886 for the Port Perry, Ont., Exhibition.

THE "St. Anne De Beaupre, P.Q.", medalets number some 18 varieties, and are quite an interesting series. They are s.ruck in silver, brass and white metal.

IN addition to the above religious medalets we would note the issue of "Ste Ann De Varennes" (a village 15 miles from Montrea¹): Reverse—a wreath of flowers. In centre "Tableau le 16 juillet. 1842, couronne." Engraved by Vachette.

THE "Vexator Canadensis" has become extremely rare and hard to procure at any price. Quite an interesting pamphlet has been written by Mr. Kingsford, of Toronto, on this rough specimen of Canadian Coinage.

FLORINS are now issued from the mints of several European countries, and differ in value, the silver florins varying from 11½d. (the lowest value) to 2s. 2d. The florin takes its name from a coin first struck at Florence, in Italy, in the twelfth century, which was noted for its beauty.

IT is stated that the rare and splendid collection of British coins, the property of the late Mr. Brice, of Bristol, has been sold for £8,000 (about $40,000) to a London connoisseur.— *Weekly Times and Echo, London, 1887.*

THE "Canadian Coin Cabinet" is the title of Dr. Leroux's new issue with 1308 cuts and 310 pages; size 5 x 8 inches.

T. is is quite a jump from some 250 pieces in the Numismatic Atlas to 1308 in "The Coin Cabinet.' (We "await with breathless expectancy its arrival.")

WHILST we cannot dictate to medalists as to what they shall or shall not use in their issues, still we would suggest that the muling of médals be avoided altogether. The value and usefulness being greatly deteriorated by this process.

MR. GOSCHEN'S jubilee sixpences are selling freely in London at 2s. 3d. In windows where these coins are exposed for sa!e, a gilded sixpence and a half-sovereign are exhibited on the same card with the question "WHICH IS WHICH?" superadded. This substantiates our statement in last month's number of this Journal that unprincipled persons would take advantage of the similarity of the gold and silver issues, and perpetrate gilded frauds. The U.S. Goverment had to recall the V. Nickel (without the word cents) for the same reason. It is a matter of surprise that the mint officials should have made such an error in the jubilee coinage.

A COIN DEALER for upward of 25 years, gives it as his opinion, that the issues of the two rare United States copper cents 1799 and 1804 were about as follows:

2500 of 1799.
1800 " 1804.

This would make the 1804 the rarest of the two dates, although, the 1799 is considered the rarest, and brings the highest price at the auction or private sale, he also adds. "During all the years of our numismatic career, and while manipulating public coin sales by auction in New York and Philadelphia, we have found three 1799 cents to two of 1804."

THE 1804 dollar quoted in our last number should have been $800 instead of $8.

DR. LEROUX writes: "I expect my book ready about the 1st of May next."

The Dr. is anxious to secure all the help he can from collectors in the shape of rubbings of coins, medals and tokens, and as he has to depend on collectors for this information we trust, all who can, will help him in his laborious undertaking The writer has already sent some 250 impressions. It is necessary that all should be in by the 1st of November, 1887.

THE first coin with the figure of Britannia on it was a large brass one, struck in the year of Rome, 874 (A.D. 121), in commemoration of the arrival of the Emperor Hadrian in Britain. Most antiquarians believe the figure to be the Province of Britain personified. It cannot be Rome, and the absence of characteristic attributes of the island is in all probability owing to the ignorance of the engraver of the die, which was doubtless not executed in Britain. There are also extant coins of Antoninus Pius, a Roman Emperor, who reigned after Hadrian, with what is supposed to be the figure of Brittania upon them. Coins bearing this figure were not struck again till the time of Charles II.

THROUGH the kindness of Sir Charles Tupper we have become the recipient of a beautiful bronze medal (secured in London for the writer). It is in bronze, by Wyon, size 33 millimetres, and is struck to comemorate the Colonial ane Indian Exhibition held in 1886. The description is as follows: Obverse, Bust of H.R H. the Prince of Wales to left, surrounded by the words, "Albert Edward Prince of Wales, Executive President." Reverse, "Colonial and Indian Exhibition, London, 1886,'. The words in fine straight lines are surrounded by a heavy wreath of oak leaves and acorns. The work is excellent; the bust on obverse standing out in fine relief, and is similar to the Canadian Thanksgiving Medal in expression. The medal will be awarded a place in "the medals of our Dominion."

THE new British coin, the double florin or dollar, is believed to be the beginning of the end of the old pounds, shillings pence and farthings division of the British money. For a long time the present pound has been regarded as an inconvenient unit of monetary value and many schemes have been proposed to remedy the fault. The London Chamber of Commerce has now under consideration a plan making the four shilling piece the unit of value or dollar, and dividing it into cents. By this plan nearly all the existing coins can be utilized without creating any confusion from having a double standard of unit value in force. The foreign will become five dollars, two shilling a half dollar, one shilling twenty-five cents, while the new coing would be ten and five cents, the new penny two cents, and the halfpenny one cent.

THE gold held by the treasury in its vaults at Washington, weights 519 tons. If packed in ordinary carts, one ton to each cart, it would make a procession two miles long, allowing twenty feet of space for the movement of each horse and cart. The silver in the same vaults, weights 7,396 tons. Measuring it in carts, as in the case of gold, it would require the services of 7,396 horses and carts to transport it, and would make a procession over twenty-one miles in length.

"THE LANGLOIS CHECK." Quite an interesting little check has turned up lately, issued by the St. Leon Water Co. The 'St Leon Sprngs" are situated in Maskinonge Co., P.Q. within easy access of Montreal and Quebec. The check is brass, and bears the name of the Co's., manager. Obverse—Crown in centre surrounded by the letters "C.E.A. Langlois" with beaded outer rim. Reverse—"Drink St. Leon Water," the first and last words are in semi, the centre word in straight line, with a star above and below, and beaded outer circle. Size 12 millimetres.

DR. LEROUX writes, my Supplement will be ready about May 1st 1888.

New Medals.

THE following is a description of three recent issues by P. W. Ellis & Co., Toronto:

1. Medals presented by the Canadian Manufacturers' Association for design, size 28. Obverse, Art as a female figure stands with wreath around her head, pointing Labor to a design which she holds with her left hand, whilst in her right she holds a pencil Labor is represented as a mechanic sitting on a stool with elbows leaning on bench, sleeves rolled up and hand resting on hammer, looking towards the design to which Art is calling his attention ; to the left of Art is a pedestal on which stands a pot containing a full blown lily bud and leaves; underneath the figures, running one third of circle, is a scroll bearing the words in raised Roman letters " Arte et labore." Reverse—In centre, a branch of three maple leaves, and on an outer rim, in raised letters the words " Canadian Manufacturers' Association." The design and execution are excellent.

2. Medal presented to the scholars of the Toronto Collegiate Institute by the trustee board, as a souvenir of the Queen's jubilee. Size 22. Obverse—(Same as the jubilee issue.) Bust of the Queen with coronated head in upper semi " Queen's Jubilee," on lower semi " Victoria Regina." Reverse—Coat of Arms of the Institute, motto on garter, " Nil decet invita minerva," surrounded by maple leaves, around outer circle (in raised letters), " Toronto Collegiate Institute." " Founded 1807."

3. The Electric Globe Battery, (in medallic shape,) is issued in combination of metals containing magnetism, and thereby supposed to cure various diseases. Size 24. Obverse—In centre, Globe encircled by the words. " Globe Electric Battery," on outer circle, " Price $1." " A. W. Burke, Toronto, Ont.," in two semis. Reverse—In centre the word, " Antimorbific;" four stars above and four below ; on outer circle, a wreath of laurel, with crown on top of circle, with the word " Health " on belt.

Discovery of Old Coins.

(*London Times, June 2nd.*)

The discovery of treasure made in Aberdeen on Monday having been brought under the notice of the Crown authorities, the Queen's remembrancer instructed the procurator fiscal of the city to claim the bronze urn and its contents on behalf of the Queen. The owner of the ground on which the find was made refused to give it up, but the authorities insisted upon it, and it has now been handed over to the Crown. The coins have been cleaned of the verdigris with which they were incrusted, and examined by numismatists, who discovered that they are of various dates and belong to various countries. English coins of the reign of Edward 1st and 2nd predominate, but there are also Scotch coins of the reigns of David and Alexander. In addition, there is a considerable number of French coins and ecclesiastical money, the latter bearing miters and staffs. The coins vary in size from a modern threepenny piece to a shilling. Twenty-two weighed an ounce, and it is calculated that the total number found was from 12,000 to 14,000 ; but a great many were removed before the finder realised their value. Several of the coins have been analysed by the Professor of Chemistry in Aberdeen University, who stated that the tolerably clean coins yielded in 100 parts 89, 88 of silver and 10, 12 of copper. The composition is therefore nearer to the French coins than those of English. The Edward coins have an inscription around the outer edge on the obscrve side, with a clear cut head bearing an open crown. On the reverse side there is also an inscription, and the coin is marked with the strongly defined cross peculiar to the quarter money. In the acute angles formed by the cross, trefoils are placed. Another coin has a crowned head in profile inclosed in a triangle on the obscrve side and an inscription, while on the reverse side, it is almost similar to that before described with the exception that stars are substituted for the trefoils.

Most of the money is of this description, but numismatists state that there are several exceedingly rare coins among the number.

It is estimated that the coins were of about the same value as sovereigns are now. There are several theories as to the circumstances under which the coins were buried, but from the dates it is conjectured that they were hidden about the time of the battle of Barra, fought near Inverurie, between the forces of Edward of England and Robert the Bruce.

The spot selected would at that date be on the Aberdeen burgh boundary, near what was known as the Ghaists' Row, on account of the supposed nightly visitation by ghosts. A bishop's residence stood near the spot, and from the fact that there was no covering on the urn it is conjectured that it was buried hurriedly during a time of panic. Another theory is that the coin formed part of the money used to pay British soldiers, and that it was left in the flight which followed the engagement with Bruce at Barra.

A CRUSHER.

I sent a letter to my love
And all my passion told,
I called her " darling," "sweetheart," " dove "—
For distance made me bold. *

I vowed to her that sad and drear
Would be my wretched life,
Unless she turned a friendly ear
And said she'd be my wife.

I begged that she would let me know
Without delay my fate.
That was a month or more ago
Still anxiously I wait.

How can my love so cruel be?
How can she try me so?
And her delay in answering me,
Does it mean " yes " or " no ?"

What's that? The bell? The postman's ring?
"A letter, sir, for you."
Ten thousand hallelujahs sing !
My darlings heart is true !

But no ! What's this ? " Your letter, sir !"—
I see beneath the lamp
The very note I wrote to her,
And mailed without a stamp!

DECEMBER 1887.

Toronto Philatelic Journal

A Monthly Magazine
For Stamp-Collectors

CANADA
NORTH
AMERICA

SOUTH
AMERICA

TORONTO PHILATELIC COMPANY,
106 HURON STREET.

TORONTO CANADA.

Toronto Philatelic Co.

106 HURON STREET,

- TORONTO

CANADA.

CHEAP SETS.

UNUSED.

	No. in sets.	Price.
Alsace and Lorraine	7	25 Cents.
Heligoland	21	40 "
" wrapper	3	10 "
Mauritius Brittaina	5	60 "
Mexico Porte de Mar colored	6	70 "

USED.

Bulgaria	6	10 "
Egypt, 1885	4	8 "
"	15	25 "
Transvaal, 1868	5	30 "
French Colonies	5	8 "
Canada Law Stamp	10	40 "

☞Stamps sent on approval to responsible parties.

THE A Packet of postage stamps, used and unused, contains 35 stamps, from Antigua, Argentine Republic, Austria, Alsace, etc.

Price, Postpaid, 25c.

TORONTO PHILATELIC CO., 106 HURON ST.

TORONTO, CANADA.

COLLECTORS

desiring rare stamps on approval will please write me. Reference required.

32 pp. Illustrrted Catalogue for stamp.

W. F. GREANY,

827 Brannan St.,

San Francisco, Cal.

SPECIALTIES!!

Nova Scotia (set of 6) 1860—1c., 2c., *5c., 8½c., 10c., and 12½c.		$1 65
Nova Scotia, 1850—3d		25
do 1860—1d		1 25
Newfoundland, 1857—8d		1 00
do 1865—5c., black		20
do 1865—24c., blue		40
*British Guiana, 1882, prov'l—12c., lilac of 1860 surch'ged 1c., official		2 50
*British Guiana, 1882, prov'l—24c., green of 1863 surch'g'd 2c., official		2 50
*British Guiana, 1882, prov'l—48c., brown of 1876 surch'ged 1c., official		1 25
*Bermuda, 1875' prov'l—3d buff, surch'ged, 1d		35
*Bermuda, 1875, prov'l—2d, blue, surch'ged, 1d		60
do 1875, " —2d, blue, " 3d. (Roman		2 50
*Nevis, 1883, prov'l—halved 1d. mauve, surch'ged, ½d, purple		1 00
do 1883, " — " " " ½d, black		50
Royal Mail Steam Packet Company, 10c., rose		75
Canada, 8c., register		30
*Macao, 1887, prov'l—3or., surch'ged 1or		15
* do " —80., " 2or.		15
Ports Rico, 1882, error—5c., yellow		1 50
do " —6d., black, " 2½d.		75
Turks Island, 1881, prov'l—1s., mauve, surch'ged 2½d.		1 55
New Brunswick (set of six) 1860—1c., 2c., 5c., 10c., 12½c., and 17c.		1 25
Prince Ed. Id. { set of 1860—2d., 3d., 4d., 4½d., 6d., and 9d.		1 00
{ " 1872—1c., 2c., 3c., 4c., 6c., and 12c. }		
Honduras Republic, 1877, prov'l—2r., green, surch'ged 1r., black		75
Honduras Republic, 1877, prov'l—2r., rose, surch'ged 2r., blue		1 00

Stamps marked * are used.

Return postage must accompany enquiries.

Choice consigments of *rarities* only sent on approval to parties making deposit.

My approval sheets are the finest in the market. Commission 25%.

The Philatelic Courier.

is published quarterly and, as it circulates in all parts of the world, it is a first-class advertising medium. Subscription $1 per annium. Advertising rates 40 cents per inch. A moderate rebate made to parties taking larger space or contracting for continued advertiseme its.

HENRY HECHLER,

Wholesale and retail dealer in

Stamps, Coins and Curiosities,

184 and 186 Argyle St.,

HALIFAX,

NOVA SCOTIA, CANADA.

I HAVE ALL values of the 1st, 2nd and 3rd issues of Canada Bill Stamps (used or unused) for cash o' good exchange. Sheets sent on approval. 100 foreign stamps (fine) for every stamp catalogue sent me. Stamps exchanged. Correspondents wanted in all foreign countries.

Address,

John R. Hooper,

Ottawa, Ontario, Canada.

Toronto Philatelic Journal.

VOL. 2.	TORONTO, DECEMBER, 1887.	No. 6.

Written for the TORONTO PHILATELIC JOURNAL.

Canadian Post Cards.

BY HENRY S. HARTE.

There exist distinct varieties of Canadian Post Cards exclusive of the varieties in color and paper.

The first card issued was in 1871, value one cent., color blue ; of this issue there are to be found two varieties,—one with name of the firm by whom they were manufactured in small capitals at the bottom of the card thus "British American Bank Note Co., Montreal and Ottawa;" the other lacking the word "Ottawa."

In 1877 a two cent card was issued, color green. This card was inscribed, "To United Kingdom" and was for use between Canada and Great Britain.

In 1879 another two cent card was put forth, also printed in green, bearing in addition to the usual matter found upon our cards the words "Union Postale Universelle" at the top of the card.

The designs of these three cards were somewhat similiar, each bore the head of the Queen, to right upon shield the words "one cent" beneath it, and on the 1879 card "Canada" at the top and "Post Card" at the bottom of the shield in small letters. The legend "Canada Post Card. The address only to be written on this side," and three blank lines prefaced by the word "To," making up the face of the card.

A new one cent card was issued in 1882, without border or address lines of 1871 card. The head of the Queen is to be found in a frame to the right, surrounded by words "Canada Postage," "one cent," numeral in a circle right and left centres.

Legend in a scroll at the top, beneath which is to be found the usual direction. "The address only to be written on this side."

A reply card, one x one cent, color slate, was also issued in 1883 of same design as the one cent card.

There was issued in 1886, a number of these cards with the head of Queen printed by mistake in the left hand corner of the card.

In 1887 the dies of the one cent and reply cards were changed. The new dies resembling that of the 1875 newsband.

The front or engraved side of the card is intended for the address only and nothing else is allowed to be written or printed upon it. It is also forbidden to attach anything to a card or to cut and alter it in any way. In case of so doing, it is not mailable as a post card.

Private post cards are not allowed to pass through the mails, nor are the cards of any British or Foreign except such be the return half of a reply card.

A treasure dating back two centuries has just been discovered in an old house, standing in a garden in the Rue Galande, Paris. The landlady was having some repairs executed and gas laid on, and the workmen, on tearing down the paper in a room on the ground floor, found, artfully concealed in a recess in the wall, an iron box containing wills and family papers, dating from the year 1694, with a quantity of coins, among which were about 160 foreign gold pieces of the size of double-louis. The next day the workmen, in digging in the garden to lay down the gas-pipes, came upon another box with 1,200 pieces of gold and silver of the same kind.

NUMISMATIC DEPARTMENT.

All correspondence in this department should be addressed to Mr. Jos. Hooper, Box 145, Port Hope.

THE question of adopting a decimal system of coinage is again attracting attention in England.

THE price now asked for the seven pieces of the silver Jubilee coins(in proof condition) is eight dollars.

IN addition to above the Maundy set of 1887 comprising 4d, 3d, 2d and 1d in silver is to hand, these are of the old type obverse and numeral reverse.

To date of writing, the five cent (silver) and one cent (copper) of 1887 is all that have turned up as new features in our Dominion coins of this year.

THE Numismatic and Antiquarian Society will hold in December, on the occasion of its twenty-fifth anniversary, a loan exhibition of Canadian historical portraits and object relating to Canadian archæology.

WE had a 1382 Nova Scotia cent offered lately, this error was committed by the die cutters. A few found their way to this country, the correction of 1832 followed. This monstrosity " the 1382 " commands quite a premium.

THE coins of the German Empire may be used also as weights. A pfennig piece weighs exactly two grams ; so does a gold five-mark piece. A nickel ten-pfennig and a ten-mark gold piece weigh each four grams.

Two BIG COPPER CENTS, issued in 1817, are among the rarest in the coin collection of the Philadelphia mint. These have the liberty heads well defined but on the top of the head over the liberty cap, is a small protuberance, which under a microscope, appears as a crown. This was cut in the die by an English engraver, who thus covertly set the British crown over the American liberty head.

THE Queen has issued an order that the Jubilee medal, of which about a thousand have been given away, is to rank above all war medals, and it is always to worn on those full-dress occasions when ordinary medals are de rigueur.

AT a dinner at Roundout, lately there was a German just arrived, who had not seen United States paper money. A gentleman opposite took a $50 bill from his pocket and endeavored to hand it to the German, but dropped it into a dish of soup. He took it out as quickly as possible and was waving it to and from to dry it, when a big dog in the room snapped it out of his fingers and bolted it down with apparent relish.

THE CHICAGO PRESS CLUB has become the possessor of a valuable historical relic in the shape of the first $5 note issued by the government. No 1. of series A. 1852. It was presented to the club by the new treasurer, George Schneider, president of the Illinois National Bank, and is valued by numismatists at $500. There has been for some years considerable speculation as to the whereabouts of this note, and its presentation to the club will settle the question of its location for all time to come

IT is said that there are only seven genuine 1804 dollars in the U.S., counterfeiters have been very successful in changing 1801 issues to that of 1804. A most ingenious mode of deception is the changing of dates of common issues of a certain coin, to the date of the year whose issue is scarce and consequently high, so that it takes an expert to distinguish them. Very lately, I had sent me what the party called an 1804 cent asking a fancy price for it, wishing to satisfy myself as to its genuiness as far as possible, I applied a strong magnifier and could distinguish easily the hollowing or easing down process, the sloping and horizontal bars having been worked out of the field. I returned it with thanks.

The death is annonnced of George Sim, (Numismatist,) Scotland. His collection of Greek and Roman coins number over 13,000, and is perhaps the finest in the world.

THE only money of Tonquin is the Tapek, a small coin of base metal resembling the Chinese cash, but only one-fourth as valuable. Forty-three of them are worth one cent. There are, therefore 4,300 in one dollar, which weighs over twenty pounds. Ten dollars make a heavy load for the stout wheel-barrows which fill the place of drays in America in doing the heay city transportation, and the pay of a regiment or two in the old days of Tong Doe rule sufficed to load a good-sized junk.

A COIN COLLECTOR in the Lower Pro vinces in search of rarities lately came across an old man who stated he had some old coins for sale, the collector, of course, asked the old gentleman if he had one with a "sheaf of wheat" on it and was told that he had—a fancy figure was offered—accepted and paid in advance with the positive understanding that he was to deliver the *rarity* that evening. judge of our numismatic friend's surprise and disgust when he was handed an English half penny *trade token*, with a sheaf on the reverse worth from five to ten cents.

THE standard of pure gold is 24 carats, coin being 22½ parts of gold and one and half parts alloy. The best jewelry running 14, 16 and 18 carats. When it is required to know the purity of any piece, a small portion is weighted and the alloy is taken out by nitric acid. The remainder is pure gold and the proportion easily found. This process is assaying. It is colored as desired by the alloy. Copper alloy makes it red, of which the English sovereign is a good specimen, and silver makes it white, like the Australian sovereign.

THE following test for deciding whether coin is good or bad is generally known as the *Mint Test*:

TEST FOR GOLD.

Strong nitric acid (36°), 30 parts ; muriatic acid, 1 part ; water, 20 parts.

TEST FOR SILVER.

Nitrate of silver, 24 grains ; nitric acid, 30 drops ; water, 1 ounce.

Use the liquids as near the edge of suspected coin as possible, as that is the part most worn. A drop of the preparation will have no effect on genuine coin. while it can be plainly seen on the counterfeit. In case the suspected coin is plated, scrape the coin a little before applying the test.

A CURIOUS MEDAL was recently found on the farm of Harrison Loring of Boston, in Duxbury, Mass. It is about an eighth of an inch greater in diameter then a silver dollar and about one half as thick. It is apparently of pewter, around the rim in Roman capital letters, a quarter of an inch high is the inscription, "Gloria in Excelsis, 1633." The last figure of the date is a little indistinct. With the lettering is a circle which encloses a winged figure rather over an inch in height. A skirt conceals the lower part of the body and limbs as far as the feet. In the right hand is a sword, and in the left something which may be a torch or a mace. The features are indiscernible. The reverse is plain and looks as if the medal had been attached to some object as an ornament. Mrs. Loring sent it to the Pilgrim Society, Plymouth where it now is. No one knows what its purpose was, but it is conjectured that it was a medal commemorative of some religious event or formed an ornament of some communion service. The spot where it was found was one where three ancient highways joined years ago. An old pewter coat button was discovered at the same time.

TORONTO
PHILATELIC JOURNAL.

Published on the 1st of every month.

Geo. A. Lowe,   **Jos . Hooper,**
Ed. Philatelic Dept.   Ed. Numismatic Dept

SUBSCRIPTION :

United States and Canada 25c. per year; Foreign Countries,
35c. per year.

Advertising Rates :

1 inch..	0 50
2 "	0 80
½ column	1 50
1 "	2 50
1 page..	4 50

10 per cent. discount on standing advts.
Copy wanted not later than the 25th.

Remit money by P.O. order, or small amounts in one or
two cent stamps.
Address all correspondence to the

Toronto Philatelic Co.

106 Huron St.   **Toronto, Canada.**

TORONTO, DECEMBER, 1887.

VOL. I.
OF
The Toronto Philatelic Journal,
BOUND IN CLOTH WITH GILT LETTERING
Post paid · · · · $2.00
Only a few copies left.

Address,   **Toronto Philatelic Co.,**
                    106 Huron St.,   Toronto, Canada.

ANENT the criticism of our contemporary the *Halifax Philatelist*, we are advised that we are in perfect order in publishing the ticket of the C.P.A. at this stage of proceedings as given in our last and present issues.

WE are glad to see that the C.P.A. is being brought to a successful issue. In deference to Mr. Hechler we may say it is an old scheme mooted by him some years ago.

BEGINNING with the New Years number the JOURNAL will be increased to double its present size, and will contain portraits of leading Canadian Philatelists, thus making it the largest and most reliable paper in the Dominion.

DON'T conduct correspondence on postal-cards. A brief business message on a postal-card is not out of the way, but a private communication on an open card is almost insulting to your correspondent. It is questionable whether a note on a postal-card is entitled to the courtesy of a response.—*Don't.*

A postoffice employee says that the gummed surface of a postage stamp should never be placed on the tongue. Moisten the other side of the stamp and the corner of the envelope or the latter only, and the stamp will stick for all it is worth.

IT is with regret we announce that Mr. John R. Hooper, Secretary *pro tem* of the Canadian Philatelic Society being down with typhoid fever. In consequence of which the the election that was to have taken place last month will not come off till late in December or early in January.

A MOTTO for a postage stamp, " A penny for your thoughts."—*Puck.*

WE had the pleasure of meeting Mr. Ketcheson at Peterboro' last week. Mr. K. is a candidate for the presidency in the C.P.A.

INCREASE your Canadian trade by advertising in the TORONTO PHILATELIC JOURNAL.

THE *Globe* says : A great craze for the collection of postage stamps has broken out in Germany. Old and young are said to be smitten with the fad.

"JUDICIOUS advertising. That is the man secret, says Robert Bonner. "I was the first to fill two, four or eight pages, of a great newspaper with my advertise. ment. It pays. If it did not I would not be able to retire to-day with the competency I have. Get the best. Then let the people know you have it."

C. P. A.

OUR TICKET.

FOR PRESIDENT.
Henry Hechler, Halifax.

FOR VICE-PRESIDENT.
Ontario—H. F. Ketcheson, Belleville.
Nova Scotia—S. DeWolf, Halifax.
Quebec—Ernest F. Wurtele, Quebec.
New Brunswick—Henry S. Harte, Petitcodiac.
Prince Edward Island—Williston Brown, Charlottetown.
Manitoba—J. H. Todd, Branbon.

FOR SECRETARY.
Jno. R. Hooper, Ottawa.

FOR TREASUSER.
T. J. McMinn, Toronto (formerly Treasurer, Toronto Philatelic Society).

EXCHANGE SUPERINTENDENT.
Fred. J. Grenny, Brantford.

EXECUTIVE COMMITTEE.
R. F. McRae, Theo. Larsen and A. E. Warren.

FOR OFFICIAL ORGAN
TORONTO PHILATELIC JOURNAL.

OFFICIAL EDITOR.
E. Y. Parker, Toronto.

LIBRARIAN.
Rev. Mr. Barnes, Montreal.

COUNTERFEIT postal cards have been discovered in Pittsburgh, Pa., which are so skilfully executed that their detection is very difficult. This is the first attempt to put spurious postal cards in circulation. It is thought they came from New York.

A NOVEL WAY OF SENDING MONEY.—Five silver dimes were recently sent to a Michigan editor on a postal card. The pieces were placed in looped slits cut into the card and held there by a thread which crossed the loops.

U. S. Foreign Mails.

INCREASE IN THE TRANSTLANTIC AND SOUTH AMERICAN CORRESPONDENCE.

N. M. Bell, Superintendent of Foreign Mails, in his annual report says:—The weights of the mails conveyed from the United States to foreign countries during the year show an increase in the transatlantic mails of 10.59 per cent. of letters and 12.35 per cent. of other articles. The mails for the Central and South American countries show an event more gratifying increase of 19.21 per cent of letters and 20.49 per cent of other articles. The Central American States show an increase of 36 per cent. The cost of the foreign mail services during the year was $437,447, of which $429,036 was compensation for sea conveyance, an increase for the year of $87,447. The report shows that the Postoffice Department has pending thirteen parcel post conventions with South and Central American States and the West Indian Islands, which it is believed will be consummated within the next few months.

R. S. HARRIS & CO.

IMPORTERS AND DEALERS IN

United States and
Foreign Postage Stamps.

———

118 SUMMIT STREET,

·

DUBUQUE, IOWA.

———

MAIL TRADE ONLY.

———

Send 2c. stamps for cheapest list yet issued. All stamps sold by us warranted genuine. We guarantee satisfaction to our patrons or refund money. Sample prices from our list.

			New	Used
Angola	1870	5 R	.02	......
"	1883	10 R.	.04	......
Argentine	1 73	90c.	......	.40
"	1878	8c. Env.	......	.05
Barbadoes	1882	4d. Reg.	.25	......
Brazil	1878	300 R.	......	.06
Bosnia	1879	25kr.	......	.13
Bolivia	1867	100c. Blue	.90	......
"	1869	50c.	.60	......
"	1871	100c.	.80	......
Cyprus	1880	1d. wrapper	.03	......
Congo	1885	50 R.	......	.12
Egypt	1884	1 Pi unpaid	......	.04
"	"	2 "	......	.04

—Unused sets—

Alsace and Lorraine	7 var.	.20
Brunswick, 1852 Env	4 "	.18
British North Burneo, ½c. to 10c.	7 "	.60
Cashmere, 1883	3 "	1.00
Heligoland, including wrapper	21 "	.33
Persia, Official	4 "	.24
Peru (Chilian arms) 1c to 1 sol	6 "	2.00
Simoor, 1885 P. to 1a	4 "	.27
U. S. Post Office Dept. complete.	10 "	2.25
" Interior " "	10 "	2.00
" Agriculture " "	9 "	3.25
" State	11 "	4.25

REMIT BY P.O. ORDER OR IN CANADA CURRENCY

Return

JANUARY   1888.

Toronto
Philatelic Journal

A Monthly Magazine for Stamp-Collectors

CANADA
NORTH AMERICA

SOUTH AMERICA

TORONTO PHILATELIC CO
106 HURON STREET.

TORONTO CANADA.

Toronto Philatelic Journal.

VOL. 2.   TORONTO, JANUARY, 1888.   No. 7.

CANADIAN PHILATELISTS.

HENRY HECHLER.

HENRY HECHLER, our candidate for the Presidency of the Canadian Philatelic Association, has earned a world-wide reputation among advanced philatelists and a sketch of his life will doubtless be of interest to our readers at the present juncture.

Mr. Hechler was born in Hesse, Darmstadt, South Germany, about 38 years ago. He was the son of General War Paymaster Wilhelm Hechler, of Darmstadt. After the usual course of study graduated, and in 1859 first became interested in philately, and founded his collection which has grown to such magnificent proportions that as long ago as 1881 he declined a cash offer of £600 sterling for it. Of course he has since then added largely to it and it now comprises over eleven thousand specimens.

In his 16th year he entered his noviciate in commerce from which he was suddenly called by the outbreak of the war of 1870-1 between his native country and France.

He served with credit throughout that campaign, taking part in many of the leading engagements of that war, such as the battles and seiges which ended in the surrender of Field Marshal Bazaine's army of 173,000 men at Metz. Also the storming of Orleans where 45,000 uninjured Frenchmen were captured. He was also actively present at the battles of Meung, Beaugency, Montlivault, Vienne and many minor affairs. At the close of the war he returned home with his regiment, the 115th Life Guards of the Grand Duke of Hesse-Darmstadt, and received the decorations for service in that war.

In 1873 he came to America, and after visiting New York, Boston and other American cities he went to Halifax where he married and has since resided. Taking the occupation of philatelic and numismatic dealer and tobacconist. His place of business is 184 Argyle Street, Halifax. where philatelists are always welcome.

Soon after settling down in Halifax he attached himself to the 63rd Rifles where his military experience served him well, for he rose rapidly till in 1881 he was gazetted as captain of No. 2 Company.

When the Halifax Provisional Battalion was formed to aid in suppressing the Indian and half-breed rebellion of 1885 Capt Hechler volunteered to go to the front and was given command of "F" Company which did service chiefly at Saskatchewan Landing. This service added the North-West medal to his other honours.

In the spring of 1887 he was elected Alderman for Ward 4 of Halifax, which is a circumstance specially worthy of note from the fact that he is the first German ever elected to that position in Halifax.

He holds the largest and most varied stock of stamps, cards, envelopes and newsbands of all countries possessed by any dealer in Canada and he does a very large wholesale and retail business in this line.

Difference in Postage Rates.

While letters posted in the Unted States are carried to any part of Canada for two cents, letters posted in Canada to any part of the United States, or even of this country, costs three cents The postage should be the same each way. It is absurd that people living in a foreign country should be able to make use of our postal facilities at a lesser rate than we can make use of them ourselves. Why this special regard for the conscience of foreigners? It is now proposed in the United States to further reduce the postage to one cent, which would entail a reduction in postal receipts of about eight millions of dollars. While that is the direction in which the postal authorities are moving on the other side of the boundary line it is interesting to observe that on this side it is seriously proposed to re-impose the postage on newspapers sent from the office of publication. In one country postal facilities are being made cheaper. In the other they are being made dearer. This is not very flattering to those who hold the reins of government in Canada, but it seems that the postmaters complain of having too much to do for the salaries they receive and that the postal department needs more revenue. Experience has shown heretofore that the lower the rate of postage exacted for carrying letters the larger the number of letters sent, and that what was lost in one way was sure to be made up in another. The tax on intelligence should be made as light and as easy to hear as possible. The re-imposition of the postal duty on newspapers is a step backwards and therefore a step in the wrong direction.

Letter Box System.

Inquiry at the Postoffices on the subject of emptying street post-boxes elicited the information that the system is most complete. As is well known the boxes in the centre of the city to the number of about two dozen searched by the "go as-you-please letter-carrier," in a large district between the centre and extreme limits the boxes are searched by waggon drvers under a Government street contract, while the extremely distant boxes are searched by the letter-carriers of the several districts in which they are situated. The constantly-made insinuation that such-and-such a box had not been visited, and the want of confidence generally in that late of letters consigned to the street letter boxes, is not much relished in the Postoffice. As long ago as 1885 Postmaster Patteson instituted a plan by which it is impossible for the drivers of the collecting waggons to miss a box. The beauty of the plan is its simplicity. It is well known that each letter-box has a case inside it into which letters drop, the case and its contents being removed bodily to the Postoffice. Each out going waggon takes out twenty-four cases with tops painted all one color, say blue. Twenty-four boxes are brought back, which are supposed to be all brown. If there is a blue one among them the driver is bound to explain. This is practically never the case except when a lock has been found frozen, and when that occurs the postoffice locksmith is sent at once to pick it. A recent invention, it is believed, will prevent the freezing of locks in future. The public may have the most implicit confidenco in the punctualits of the search made of the street letter-boxes.

The New York Sun suggests that it would be a memorable rounding out of the first century of legislation under the American Union, for Congress to establish one cent letter postage throughout the United States. The country would then have the cheapeat mail rates in the world.

NUMISMATIC DEPARTMENT.

All correspondence in this department should be addressed to Mr. Jos. Hooper, Box 145, Port Hope.

FOR information about coins, go to a connoisseur, of course.

CROWN pieces to the value of twenty million maks will shortly be struck off in Germany.

THE English guinea was first coined in 1673, and derived its name from the fact that the gold of which it was at first composed came from Guinea.

THE Bank of France has found a valuable detective agent in photography, suspected coins are photographed with genuine ones, and the counterfeits are revealed by comparison.

THE coins of the German Empire may be used also as weights. A pfennig piece weights exactly two grams; so does a gold five mark piece. A nickel ten-pfennig and a ten-mark gold piece weights each four grams.

AN extensive robbery has been committed at Athens at the Numismatic Museum, attached to the University. Amongst the articles stolen are a quantity of gold coins of the Quintus Flaminius series, a number of Attic tetradrachms, including the well-known Mithridates Aristion series of the town of Asia Minor, and also several Ætolian tetradrachms.

INASMUCH as considerable misapprehension exists as to the precise value of the distinction conferred by the possession of a Jubilee medal, it may be well to state that the Jubilee medal ranks next to the decorations to the various Orders, and takes precedence of all naval, military, and other medals.

THE secretary to the Queen's Remembrancer, Edinburgh, has been directed to pay in equal proportions to James Bisset, William Hay, Alexander Fraser, and John Urquhart, the finders of the bronze pot and cons in Upper Kirkgate, Aberdeen, about eighteen months ago, the sum of £139 17s, 6d, the value of the tressure tove.

TORONTO
PHILATELIC JOURNAL.

Published on the 1st of every month.

Geo. A. Lowe,   **Jos . Hooper,**
ED. PHILATELIC DEPT.   ED. NUMISMATIC DEPT

SUBSCRIPTION :

United States and Canada 25c. per year ; Foreign Countries, 35c. per year.

Advertising Rates :

1 inch	0 50
2 "	0 80
½ column	1 50
1 "	2 50
1 page	4 50

10 per cent. discount on standing advts.

Copy wanted not later than the 25th.

Remit money by P.O. order, or small amounts in one or two cent stamps.

Address all correspondence to the

Toronto Philatelic Co.

106 Huron St.   **Toronto, Canada.**

TORONTO, JANUARY, 1888.

VOL. I.
OF
The Toronto Philatelic Journal.
BOUND IN CLOTH WITH GILT LETTERING
Post paid · · · · $2.00

Only a few copies left.

Address,   **TORONTO PHILATELIC CO.**,
106 HURON ST.,   TORONTO, CANADA

THE U. S. ocean mail contract will not be decided until the return of the Post-master-General from Washington.

WILLIAM M. PUNSHON was almost a monomanac in collecting autographs. He left about 1,500, comprising those of the most famous persons in the world.

BATCHELDER's new 32 page catalogue of postage stamps is to hand. It presents a fine appearance, and prices are unusually low.

WE beg to call attention to the advertisement of W. J. Parrish in another column. His 25c. packet of U. S. stamps,

containing 50 varieties are of special value. It contains the 1870—3c. grilled, special delivery, 2c. P.O. envelope, a Plimpton envelope, etc.

IT is stated that the Atlantic mail contract, now held by the Allans, and for the renewal of which the Allans, Dominion line, Canada Atlantic Company, and Anderson & Co. tendered, will certainly go to Anderson & Co., the representatives of the Canadian Pacific Railway.

POSTMASTER-GENERAL MCLELAN says the Parcels' Post Treaty with the States will go into effect February 1st. The rates are not yet fixed. He says regarding the rumor that the Government would impose postage on newspapers that the Government are considering how to stop the abuse of postal privileges by advertising agents and others who send posters and flysheets through the mails as newspapers. Exactly how to attack this abuse the Government has not decided.

A WOMAN died in Washington last week from the effects of poison in the ink used in printing greenbacks. She was employed in the Bureau of Engraving and Printing as an assistant to a pressman, and, while handling sheets of bills with the fresh green ink upon them, inhaled the poisonous matter and acquired a disease from which she never recovered.

THE cheapest way to paper a room is to use postage stamps obtained from all your friends. It only requires 33,542 to paper a small room. An expeditious way is to advertise for a genteel governess, or a dry goods clerk (salary $2,000 a year), and you will have sufficient stamps to paper your largest room, and a closet to spare.

Stamp Collection in Education.

A perfect craze has sprung up in Germany for the collection of postage-stamps, and it is not by any means confined, as is largely the case in England, to boys, but extends to grown-up people engaged in various walks of life, post-office and other officials, etc. Dr. von Stephan thinks that if young men became interested in foreign postage-stamps they will at the same time take interest in the countries whence the stamps comes. Stamp-collecting is, therefore, to be the future royal road to the learning of geography and a means of commercial education.

Striving to Please.

Old lady (sharply, to boy in drug store) —I've been waitin' for some time to be waited on, boy.

Boy (meekly)—Yes'um ; wot kin I do for you ?

Old lady—I want a two-cent stamp.

Boy (anxious to please)—Yes'um. Will you have it licked ?

FRED. GRENNY,

Member of C.P.A. and A.P.A., Brantford, Ont., Can.,

DEALER IN

Canada and Foreign Postage Stamps.

Canadian Coins and Medals a specialty. Old stamps of any country wanted. Fine approval sheets at 25 per cent. commission sent to parties furnishing good reference. Complete set of unused Canada post cards. Nine var. for 60 cts.

Complete set, 13 var. unused, P.E.I....	$1 25	
" 3 " " Canada Reg....	30	
" " " 1882, Nicaragua ...	80	
Set of 5 unused, 1c., 2c., 10c., 20c. First issue perf. and 20c. rouletted. Nicaragua	80	
Brant Memorial medals, each	25	

BELOW IS OUR ADDRESS

IF YOU DESIRE GENUINE

STAMPS AT LOW PRICES.

THE BROOKLYN STAMP CO., P.O. Box 7, Brooklyn,N.Y.

Toronto Philatelic Co.

106 HURON STREET,

- TORONTO

CANADA.

CHEAP SETS.

UNUSED.

	No. in sets.	Price.
Alsace and Lorraine	7	25 Cents.
Heligoland	21	40 "
" wrapper	3	10 "
Mauritius Brittaina	5	60 "
Mexico Porte de Mar colored	6	70 "

USED.

Bulgaria	6	10 "
Egypt, 1885	4	8 "
"	15	25 "
Transvaal, 1869	5	30 "
French Colonies	5	8 "
Canada Law Stamp	10	40 "

☞Stamps sent on approval to responsible parties.

COLLECTORS

desiring rare stamps on approval will please write me. Reference required.

32 pp. Illustrated Catalogue for stamp.

W. F. GREANY,

327 Brannan St.,

San Francisco, Cal.

BUY NOW CHEAP.

7. Mexico	10	*Canada, 8cts. Register	...	13
4. Orange States	06	*Br. Borneo, 23c		45
6. South America	05	Mexico, 1872, 100cts		20
20. " "	25	Nova Scotia, 3 pence		25
3. Mexico, 1856	35	" " 5 cents		05
Guatemala, 1886—(150c.); provisional	40			
Peru, 1 sol unused, or 50 cts. unpaid, 1883, surcharged	90			

∴Unused.

Sheets on approval, 33⅓%

Lists free or with 50 stamps, 2cts.

ROBERT F. McRAE, C.P.A. 6.

573 ST. URBAIN ST.,   MONTREAL.

SPECIALTIES!!

Nova Scotia (set of 6) 1860—1c., 2c., *5c., 8½c., 10c., and 12½c.		$1 65
Nova Scotia, 1850—3d		25
do 1860—1d		1 25
Newfoundland, 1857—8d		1 00
do 1865—5c., black		20
do 1865—24c., blue		40
*British Guiana, 1882, prov'l—12c., lilac of 1860 surch'ged 1c., official		2 50
*British Guiana, 1882, prov'l—24c., green of 1863 surch'g'd 2c., official		2 50
*British Guiana, 1882, prov'l—40c., brown of 1876 surch'ged 1c., official		1 25
*Bermuda, 1875, prov'l—3d buff, surch'ged, 1d		35
*Bermuda, 1875, prov'l—2d, blue, surch'ged, 1d		60
*Nevis, 1883, prov'i—halved 1d. mauve, surch'ged, ½d, purple		1 00
do 1883, " " " " ½d, black		50
Royal Mail Steam Packet Company, 10c., rose		75
Canada, 8c., register		30
*Macao, 1887, prov'l—8or., surch'ged 10r		30
* do " " —80., " 20r		30
∴ do " " —5 on 80		50
∴ do " " —5 on 100		60
∴ do " " —10 on 200		75
Ports Rico, 1882, error—8c., yellow		1 50
Turks Island, 1881, prov'l—1s., mauve, surch'ged 2½d		1 55
do " " —6d., black, " 2½d		75
New Brunswick (set of six) 1860—1c., 2c., 5c., 10c., 12½c., and 17c.		1 25
Prince Ed. Id. { set of 1860—2d., 3d., 4d., 4½d., 6d., and 9d. { 1872—1c., 2c., 3c., 4c., 6c., and 12c.		1 00
Honduras Republic, 1877, prov'l—2r., green, surch'ged 1r., black		75
Honduras Republic, 1877, prov'l—2r., rose, surch'ged 2r., blue		1 00

Stamps marked * are used.

Return postage must accompany enquiries.

Choice consignments of *rarities only* sent on approval to parties making desposit.

My approval sheets are the finest in the market. Commission 25%.

The Philatelic Courier

is published quarterly and, as it circulates in all parts of the world, it is a first-class advertising medium. Subscription $1 per annum. Advertising rates 40 cents per inch. A moderate rebate made to parties taking larger space or contracting for continued advertisements.

HENRY HECHLER,

Wholesale and retail dealer in

Stamps, Coins and Curiosities,

184 and 186 Argyle St.,

HALIFAX,

NOVA SCOTIA. CANADA.

I HAVE ALL values of the 1st, 2nd and 3rd issues of Canada Bill Stamps (used or unused) for cash or good exchange. Sheets sent on approval. 100 foreign stamps (fine) for every stamp catalogue sent me. Stamps exchanged. Correspondents wanted in all foreign countries.

Address,

John R. Hooper,

Ottawa. Ontario. Canada.

R. S. HARRIS & CO.

IMPORTERS AND DEALERS IN

United States and
Foreign Postage Stamps.

118 SUMMIT STREET,

DUBUQUE, IOWA.

MAIL-TRADE ONLY.

Send 2c. stamps for cheapest list yet issued. All stamps sold by us warranted genuine. We guarantee satisfaction to our patrons or refund money. Sample prices from our list.

			New	Used
Angola	1870	5 R.	.02	.....
"	1883	10 R.	.04	.....
Argentine	1873	90c.	.....	.40
"	1878	8c. Env.	.....	.05
Barbadoes	1884	4d. Reg.	.25	.....
Brazil	1878	300 R.	.....	.00
Bosnia	1879	25kr.	.....	.13
Bolivia	1867	100c. Blue	.90	.....
"	1869	50c.	.00	.....
"	1871	100c.	.80	.....
Cyprus	1880	1d. wrapper	.03	.....
Congo	1886	50 R.	.....	.12
Egypt	1884	1 Pi unpaid	.....	.04
"	"	2 "	.....	.04

—Unused sets—

Alsace and Lorraine		7 var.	.20
Brunswick, 1852 Env		4 "	.18
British North Burneo, ½c. to 10c.		7 "	.00
Casmire, 1883		3 "	1.00
Heligoland, including wrapper		21 "	.33
Persia, Official		4 "	.24
Peru (Chilian arms) 1c to 1 sol		6 "	2.00
Simoor, 1885 P. to 1a		4 "	.27
U. S. Post Office Dept. complete		10 "	2.25
" Interior "		10 "	2.00
" Agriculture "		9 "	3.25
" State	1c. to 90c.	11 "	4.25

REMIT BY P.O. ORDER OR IN CANADA CURRENCY

FEBRUARY   1888.

Toronto
Philatelic Journal

A Monthly Magazine For Stamp Collectors

TORONTO PHILATELIC CO
106 HURON STREET.

TORONTO CANADA.

Toronto Philatelic Journal.

OFFICIAL ORGAN OF CANADIAN PHILATELIC ASSOCIATION

| VOL. 2 | TORONTO, FEBRUARY, 1888. | NO. 8. |

OUR CANADIAN PHILATELISTS.

JOHN REGINALD HOOPER, the promoter and organizer of the Canadian Philatelic Association, is an English-Canadian. He is a son of Joseph Hooper, Esq., the well-known marble and granite dealer, of Port Hope, Ont. The subject of our sketch was born in 1859, and is therefore nearly 29 years of age. From boyhood he evinced a military spirit which pervaded his ancestors, one of whom was owner and commander of a successful privateer in the service of King George III. At the age of 18 he passed a military examination and was appointed a sergeant in a garrison artillery battery. Attending the Royal School of Gunnery he obtained a first-class military certificate, and was a volunteer for the Cape Mounted Rifles during the Zulu campaign. Altogether he has seen nearly six years of active regular service. He served on Col. William's staff with the Midland Battalion during the North-West Rebellion, and was with General Middleton's column, participating actively in the four days'

action at Batoche, and final charge and capture of the rebel stronghold; afterwards he was on the column in the celebrated Big Bear chase in the wilderness north of Fort Pitt and Frog Lake, where he received a touch of malaria by sleeping in muskeg swamps. On his arrival back he was presented with a gold medal by admiring friends, also the Queen's medal and the " Saskatchewan " clasp for being under fire. Mr. Hooper now devotes his military ardor to a fancy drill canton of which he is 1st lieutenant.

In conjunction with his military duties he also trained as an athlete, and is the possessor of some fine medals and cups. He is credited with doing 100 yards in 10 seconds in 1883 on the historic Plans of Abraham, Quebec. He has been selected four times for competition teams in shifting heavy ordnance and big gun competitions. He has also won the championship half-mile snow race for Quebec.

Mr. Hooper's philatelic experience began in 1871, but sold his collection in

1877. He commenced collecting again in 1877, and now has nearly 8,000 specimens. He published an amateur stamp paper in 1876-7 and a society journal in 1887, principally for the purpose of booming his C.P.A. scheme. He is now a permanent Government employee in the Post Office Savings Bank at Ottawa.

For the TORONTO PHILATELIC JOURNAL.

C.P.A. OFFICIAL NEWS.

THE SECRETARY'S REPORT.

The following is the report of the Secretary *pro tem*, Mr. John R. Hooper :

To the Members of the C.P.A.

GENTLEMEN,—I have the honor to herewith present my report of the progress and organization of the C.P.A. While I have labored under some difficulties in organizing the association, I am amply repaid for my efforts from the large number of expressions of good-will which I received during my late severe sickness. I am glad that my efforts were not only successful, but the fact that we have reached a formidable number and the composition of our society ensures us continued success for the future. I first conceived the idea of forming a Canadian Stamp Association some ten years ago, but was never able to cope with the difficulties in the way, in fact my schemes were looked on coldly, and I could not secure support in the right direction. In May of last year I started a paper ostensibly to be a society magazine, *The Gossip*, but the real design of this paper was to reach the first families in Canada, and to work the C.P.A. scheme, through this means reaching our best philatelists. I sunk $200 in the enterprise by issuing three numbers, but

have the happiness to say that my scheme worked wonderfully, and a large number of older philatelists joined.

I formed a Board of Organization in June, consisting of Messrs. Grenny, Ketcheson, Leighton, McRae and Niesser. To these gentlemen I am particularly indebted to for their material assistance Our membership increased as follows : June, 9 ; July, 14 ; Aug. 10 ; Sept., 11 ; Oct., 23 ; Nov., 22 ; Dec., 5 ; Jan., 14. —Total, 108. The small number joining in December may be due to the fact that I was unable to attend to any philatelic matters during that month.

The membership roll shows the number to be residents of Ontario, 34 ; Quebec, 5 ; Nova Scotia, 24 ; New Brunswick, 2 ; P. E. Island, 1 ; Manitoba, 4 ; British Columbia, 1 ; United States, 33 ; England, Germany, Guatemala, each one, or

Canada........ 71
United States 33
Foreign....................... 5
─────
Total membership......108

The ages of the members are as follows : Under 20, 35 ; 20 to 25 years, 25 ; 25 to 30 years, 22 ; 30 to 40 years, 15 , over 40, 6 ; age not given, 5.

The occupations are variously given and quite interesting : Accountants, 2 ; agents (express) 1 ; broker, 1 ; booksellers, 2 ; bookkeepers, 8 ; civil service (Canada), 7 ; civil engineer, 1 ; clerks, 15 ; contractor, 1 ; cutter, 1 ; commercial travellers, 3 ; chemist, 1 ; carpenter, 1 ; cashier, 1 ; elocutionist, 1 ; engraver, 1 ; farmer, 1 ; gentlemen 3 ; insurance, 4 ; jeweller, 1 ; lawyers, 2 ; medicos, 2 ; machinist, 1 ; minister, 1 ; merchants, 5 ; notary, 2 ; publishers, 2 ; printers, 2 ; stamp dealers, 4 ; students, 11 , salesman, 1 ; stenographer, 1 ; town clerk, 1 ; teachers, 2 ; watchmaker, 1 ; weaver, 1.

In classifying the different occupations one of the members, I see, under this head marks "loafing." Should the members know him probably they would justify me in classing him as I did under the head of "gentlemen."

Mr. Grenny informs me he will get the Exchange Department in order as soon as possible. In this respect we will copy the A.P.A. I would suggest to the Executive Committee that they use Ketcheson's price list for Canadian stamps, and Scott's for United States and foreign in the marking of sheets by members.

The Organizing Board voted me a salary of $10, but as I left the situation after serving nine months, I suppose I have forfeited my right to any of it, so I will not claim it.

I hope all members will forward any old books or papers relating to philately to Mr. George Walker, the Librarian, of Peterboro, Ont., and we can thus get the necleus of a good start.

As Mr. Todd as left Manitoba for British Columbia, and resigned the vice-presidency, I would suggest that he be made vice-president of British Columbia and the North West Territories. Mr. Davison, of Brandon, is Mr. Todd's nominee, and I hope that the Executive Committee will appoint him to the vacancy.

The yearly fee, now due, $1.00, but which can be paid half yearly, should be sent at once to the Secretary, who will issue cards of membership as soon as printed.

The receipts of the association have been $27.75, and the expenditure $33.86, which is very light considering the amount of correspondence done and material bought. I have kept accurate accounts of all receipts and disbursements, and have on hand a good supply of stationery, books, etc., for future work. The expenditure includes the purchase of fyles for Association's papers, printing, blank and record books, postage, stationery, telegrams, binders, etc., etc. The material and itemized accounts, books, with everything belonging to the Association will be sent to Mr. J. A. Leighton, Orangeville, who will in future attend to the correspondence. The amount of receipts is from entrance fees, but the discounts on American silver, postage stamps, etc., is charged to expenditure, as I credited over 30 of our American friends with 25 cts. whereas I only could get 20 cts. each for their "quarters." Some United States members sent postal notes which are not receivable here and these had to be sent to the States to be "cashed." As a large proportion of the members remitted in postage stamps they were used on the society's correspondence. My books show the Association in debt $6.11, but I will personally reduce this to me, and hand over the books balanced. During my illness I had to secure help to desprtch the work promptly, requiring 10 to 30 answers per day.

In conclusion, I hope every member will do his utmost for the Association, and that harmony will reign supreme.

And now, gentlemen, thanking you one and all, for your kind and liberal support I still remain

JOHN R. HOOPER.

OTTAWA, Feb. 4, 1888.

MR. E. E. BOOK, publisher of the *Niagara Falls Philatelist* is about to remove to the United States, all advertisements will be filled by the TORONTO PHILATELIC JOURNAL.

HEREAFTER the subscription price of the JOURNAL will be, Canada and United States, 35 cts per year ; foreign counties, 50 cts.

TORONTO
PHILATELIC JOURNAL.

Published on the 1st of every month.

Geo. A. Lowe,   **Jos . Hooper,**
ED. PHILATELIC DEPT.   ED. NUMISMATIC DEPT

SUBSCRIPTION :

United States and Canada 25c. per year ; Foreign Countries,
35c. per year.

Advertising Rates :

1 inch	0 50
2 "	0 80
½ column	1 50
1 "	2 50
1 page	4 50

10 per cent. discount on standing advts.

Copy wanted not later than the 25th.

Remit money by P.O. order, or small amounts in one or two cent stamps.

Address all correspondence to the

Toronto Philatelic Co.

106 Huron St.   Toronto, Canada.

TORONTO, FEBRUARY, 1888.

OFFICIAL news has necessitated the leaving out of our Numismatic Department and many other interesting articles, which will however appear in our large number next month.

WE beg to thank the members of the C.P.A. for the honour they have conferred upon us by electing us as Official Organ of the C.P.A. It will always be our aim to further the interests of the society in every way that lies in our power. Our next number will be double the present size, and will combine the *Niagara Falls*

Philatelist. Any other papers wishing to have their subscription lists and advertising contracts filled will please note our address.

For TORONTO PHILATELIC JOURNAL.

Result of Elections.

LIST OF OFFICERS FOR THE C.P.A.

We, the undersigned Committee on Elections appointed by the Organizing Board to act as Scrutineers, declare the result of the ballot to be as indicated below, and that those receiving the majority of votes are hereby duly elected to fill the various offices till the next election. The amount of annual dues will be $1.00, payable in advance yearly or half-yearly. The Executive Board will select a Counterfeit Detector and Purchasing Agent, having regard to the choice of the members as expressed in their votes for these offices.

We have exercised great care in counting the ballots, and the fact that there were no spoiled ballots rendered it easier for us to give a complete return of every vote polled.

JOHN R. HOOPER.
F. J. GRENNY.
J. A. LEIGHTON.

Total membership	108
" Ballots issued	104
Foreign non-voters	4
Votes polled	96
" unpolled	8

The following is a correct and revised return of the ballots cast which is declared to be true, according to the ballots received :

FOR PRESIDENT.

H. F. Ketcheson	58
Henry Hechler	38

FOR SECRETARY.

J. A. Leighton 71
J. R. Hooper (withdrew)* ... 19

FOR TREASURER.

H. L. Hart...................... 58
T. J. McMinn 35

VICE-PRESIDENT.

Ontario { John R. Hooper 77
        { H. F. Ketcheson* 4
Quebec { R. F. McRae 48
       { E. F. Wurtele........... 28
N. Scotia { A. J. Craig 47
          { I. N. Crane............... 37
N. Brunswick { H. S. Harte...... 67
             { C. E. Willis* ... 5
P. E. I.—W. Brown 63
Manitoba { J. H. Todd 60
         { J. R. Davidson*...... 2
Exchange Supt.—F. J. Grenny... 81

FOR LIBRARIAN.

Geo. Walker 51
E. A. Smith 42
H. Mathers 1

FOR OFFICIAL ORGAN.

Toronto Philatelic Journal...... 49
Halifax Philatelist 40
Niagara Falls Philatelist......... 6
Canadian Philatelist............ ... 1

EOR OFFICIAL EDITOR.

E. Y. Parker 42
Theo. Larsen..................... 38
H. E. French........ 6
E. E. Book...................... 5

EXECUTIVE COMMITTEE.

Findlay 56
McRae 53
Niesser....... 40
King 39
Book 39
Willis 21
McMinn *(not a candidate)   4
Hooper *(not a candidate)..   4

COUNTERFEIT DETECTOR.

DeWolf........ 12
Hechler 8
Lowe 5

Messrs. Bradt, Ketcheson, Parker, French, H. S. Harte, H. L. Hart, R. A. B. Hart, and Dr. Book, .each received one vote.

PURCHASING AGENT.

E. Y. Parker...................... 4
Hy. Hechler 2
Theo. Larsen............ 2
J. R. Findlay..................... 2
Geo. A. Lowe 2
Messrs. DeWolf, Hooper, Creed, Dr. Book, H. L. Hart, and E. E. Book each received one vote.

[THE ANNUAL FEE]

For $1 ...:........ 50
"   2 18
"   1.50 17
"   .50 4

One vote each for 75c. and $10, and several agree to abide with the majority.
*Those names marked with an asterisk were not on the ballots.

To the TORONTO PHILATELIC JOURNAL Official Organ C.P.A.

I HAVE received the following from Mr. McRae, which explains itself :

J. R. HOOPER, Ottawa—

I resign the position of Vice-President of Quebec in favor of Mr. Wurtele. I had not intention of holding office, but I will remain on the Executive Committee.—
Yours truly.   ROBT. F. McRAE.
Montreal, Feb. 8, 1888.

The Executive Committee is therefore Messrs. Findlay, McRae and Niesser. Mr. Wurtele being declared Vice-President of Quebec.

JNO. R. HOOPER.

For the TORONT · PHILATELIC JOURNAL.

C.P.A. ROLL OF MEMBERS.

1—J R Hooper, 295 Albert St., Ottawa, Can.
2—F J Grenny, Brantford, Ont.
3—J A Leighton, Box 194, Orangeville, Ont.
4—H F Ketcheson, Box 499, Belleville, Ont.

5—J C Niesser, Toronto, Ont.
6—R F McRae, 573 St. Urban St., Montreal, Que.
7—G H Harrison, 629 Dufferin Av., London, Ont.
8—J H Todd, Hector, B.C.
9—Ernest F Wurtele, 93 St. Peter St., Quebec.
10—H S Harte, Petitcodiac, N. B.
11—F E Book, Niagara Falls, South, Ont.
12—H A Simpson,Belleville, Ont.
13—N E Carter, Box 314, Delevan, Wis.
14—H E French, Box 60, Niagara Falls South.
15— C E Willis, Box 140, Petitcodiac,N B
16—A J Craig, Box 20 Pictou, N.S.
17 -John R. Findlay, Box 185, Halifax. N. S.
18—Donald A King, Halifax. N. S.
19— F O Creed, 6 Smith St., Halifax,N.S
20 – Olof Larsen, 40 Lockman St., Halifax, N.S.
21—S DeWolf, Box 219 Halifax, N.S.
22—H L Hart, Box 23, Halifax, N.S.
22 –Theo Larsen, 40 Lockman St., Halifax, N.S.
24— Henry Hechler, 184 Argyle St.,Halifax, N.S.
25— H Matthews, Box 573, Halifax, N.S.
26.—C G Woodworth, Box 3003, Denver, Col.
27 –Williston Brown, P O Dept., Charlottetown, P E I
28—Frank C Kaye, Halifax, N S.
29—J. M. Sheridan, 22 St. Felix St, Brooklyn, N Y
30—E F Smith, 89 Spring Garden Road, Halifax, N S
31—J A Caron, 331 Superior St. W Duluth, Minn.
32—J J Palma, Jr, Biblioteca Nacional, Guatemala.
33—Geo A Lowe, 105 Huron St., Toronto. Ont.
34—Edmund A Smith, 58 Robie St., Halifax, N S
35—A Lohmeyer, 933 Milton Place, Baltimore, Md.
36—P F O'Keefe, Mansfield Valley Pa
37—Wilson Wilby, 106 Yorkville Av, Toronto.
38—H C. Beardsley, 422 N 7th St St. Joseph, Mo.
39—M E Deats, Flemington, N J
40—F. W Voute, 307 Webster Avenue, Chicago.
41—Rudolf Wohlfahrt, Erfurt. Germany.
42—P M Wolsieffer, 162 State St,Chicago, Illinois.
43—W S McLean,Neil's harbor, Victoria, N.S
44—C Wesley Price, Paymouth, Wayne Co, Mich.
45—W D Boyd, Box 184 Simcoe, Ont.
46—A E Warren, Box 1981, Montreal, Que.
47—S B Bradt, 225, Dearborn St., Chicago, Ill.
48—C R Gadsden, Grand Crossing, Ill.
49—W F Dent, 192 S. Division St., Buffalo, N.Y.
50—G A Haskell, 3756, Johnson Place, Chicago, Ill
51—Dudley Holmes, Goderich, Ont.
52—A Liebetrau, Gablonz, Bohemia.
53—R A Baldwin Hart, 368 Sherbrooke St., Montreal, Que.
54—J R Davidson, Brandon, Manitoba.
55—Karl C. Miner, Hoosick Falls, N. Y.
56—H R Ledyard, 108 Bloor St. W., Toronto.
57—T Burnett, Brantford, Ont.
58—Geo Walker, Peterboro, Ont.
59—J Willis Caldwell, 136 Spring Garden Road, Halifax, N.S.
60—Walter E. Simpson, Guysboro, N.S.
61—A Melvin Jones, Hoosick Falls, N.Y
62—H C. Kendall, Box 5, Emmets'urg Iowa.
63—Chas W Peugh, Kossouth, Indiana.
64—Dr. F E Book. Niagara Falls South, Ont.
65—Rev Wm Barnes, 118 Union Av, Montreal.
66—T J McMinn, 102 Rose Av., Toronto.
67—Ed Y Parker, 47 Huron St., Toronto.

68—J E. Gass, 208. Argyle St., Halifax, Nova Scotia.
69—E J Phillips, 28 Boswell Av, Toronto, Ont.
70—Mrs Julia S Mason, 362 Yonge St., Toronto, Ont.
71—E G Shannon, 58 Spring Garden Road, Halifax.
72—E R Aldrich, Benson, Minn.
73—L W Edwards, Smith's Mills, Pa.
74—Frank Rounsfell, Brandon, Manitoba
75—J H Johnson, 36 Portland St., Southport, England.
76—W D B Spry, Box 223, Barrie, Ont.
77—A E Smith, Box 562, Halifax, N. S.
78—C A Curry, 83 Morris St., Halifax, Nova Scotia
79—W L Emory, 85 High St., Fitchburg, Mass.
80—J N Crane, Box 534, Halifax, N. S.
81—F Russell, Jr., Brandon, Manitoba.
82—Alvah Davison, Helmetta, N.J., U.S.
83—E P Lea, 26 Bloor St. West, Toronto.
84—J F Macdonald, Paris, Ont.
85—J M Douglas, Jr., Middletown, Conn.
86—H Andrews, 20 Buckingham Street, Halifax.
87—G H Cox, 9 Dresden Row, Halifax.
88—Charless S Meek, 12 North Street, Toronto.
89—W J Graydon, Streetsville, Ont.
90—E Coleman, Box 1606 Portsmouth, N. H.
91—Max Stadie, 2079 2nd Av, New York
92—A G A Fletcher, Box 568 Woodstock, Ont.
93—E O Evans, Charlestown, Mass.
94—A E Williams, Killarney, Manitoba.
95—J A. Craig, Yarmouth, N.S.
96—J C Spence, Box 175 St. Marys, Ont
97—F B Eldredge, Box 705, Attleboro, Mass.
98—F Ineson, Box 563, Weston, Ont.
99—G W Von Utassy, 5055 Green St., Germantown, Pa.
100—G F Read, 9 Custom House Street, Providence, R. I.
101—V Gurd, Jr., Galveston, Texas.
102—W H Gardiner, 179 Richmond St. W., Toronto.

103—J E Skeele, Niagara Falls South, Ont.
104—Robt C H Brock, Box 287 Philadelphia.
105—Jos J Casey, 42 E 112th Street, New York.
106—Jos Ineson, Weston, Ont,
107—C A Townsend, Arkon, Ohio.
108—A G Needham, Milton, Ont.

For TORONTO PHILATELIC JOURNAL.

The C.P.A. Officers.

BY CANADENSIS.

The following is a short sketch of some of the officers elected to serve the C.P.A. for 1888:

Henry F. Ketcheson (President) was born in 1863, and is therefore about 25 years of age. He is an enthusiastic collector, a gentleman of honor and respectability; is employed in the Civil Service Post Office Department. He will make a capital man to push the C.P.A. matters.

J. A. Leighton (Secretary), of Orangeville, is an earnest worker in the ranks of philately. All who have had anything to bring them in contact with him pronounce him thoroughly fit for the office of Secretary. He is a law student.

H. L. Hart (Treasurer) is a prominent boot and shoe merchant of Halifax. He is reliable and trustworthy and he will be a good custodian of the society's funds. He is 23 years of age.

Robert F. McRae (Vice-President of Quebec) is an experienced stenographer and phonographer of Montreal. Although only 20 years of age he has "an old head on young shoulders."

A. J. Craig (Vice-President N.S.) is an old philatelist, although only 31 years of age. His residence is at Pictou, but he is a commercial traveller and makes frequent trips to all parts of the province. He is peculiarly well fitted for the position to which he has been elected.

Rev. Henry S. Harte, of Petitcodiac (Vice-President, N.B.) is a young clergyman of ability. He is a sincere and painstaking worker for the C.P A. He is 23 years of age.

J. S. Willston Brown, of Charlottetown, is the Vice-President for Prince Edward Island He is an honourable member of the Canadian Civil Service, Post Office Department and is 25 years of age.

J. H. Todd, who has been elected Vice-President for Manitoba, is now the C.P.R. station agent at Hector, British Columbia, near the Rocky Mountains. His specialty is Canada and the United States.

Fred. J. Grenny, the newly elected Exchange Superintendent, is one of the most popular collectors in Canada. He has one of the finest, if not the best, collection in the Dominion. He is also a member of the Civil Service, being Assistant Postmaster at Brantford. His age is 47, and being an old collector his experience has been large and will be of great use to the C.P.A.

George Walker (Librarian) of Peterboro, Ont., is 32 years of age. He takes a great interest in stamp collecting and will no doubt guard well the responsible trust of the new position he now occupies.

When answering Advertisements please mention this paper.

SPECIALTIES!

Nova Scotia (set of 6) 1860—1c., 2c., *5c., 8½c., 10., and
  12½c...$1 65
Nova Scotia, 1850—3d... 25
  do   1860—1d.. 1 25
Newfoundland, 1857—3d.. 1 00
  do   1865—5c.,black.. 20
  do   1865—24c., blue 40
*British Guiana, 1882, prov'l—12c., lilac 1860 surch'ged
  1c., official 2 50
*British Guiana, 1882, prov'l—24c., green of 1863 surch'g'd
  2c., official... 2 50
*British Guiana, 1882, prov'l—40c., brown of 1876 sur-
  ch'ged 1c., official 1 25
*Bermuda, 1875, pro'l—3d buff, surch'ged, 1d 35
*Bermuda, 1875, prov'l—2d, blue, surch ged, 1d 60
*Nevis, 1883, prov'l—halved 1d, mauve, surch ged, ½d,
  purple.. 1 00
  do 1883,   "   —   "   "   ½d,
  black 50
Royal Mail Steam Packet Company, 10c , rose............... 75
Canada, 8c., register... 30
*Macao, 1887, prov'l—30r., surch'ged 10r...................... 30
*   do   "   "   —80.,   "   20r...................... 30
*   do   "   "   —on 80 50
*   do   "   "   —on 100................................. 60
*   do   "   "   —on 100................................. 75
Porto Rico, 1882, error—5c., yellow................................... 1 50
Turks sland, 1881, prov'l—1s., mauve, surch'ged 2½d... 1 50
  do   "   "   —5d., black,   "   2½... 75
New Brunswick (set of six) 1860—1c., 2c., 5c., 10c , 12½c.
  and 17c... 1 25
Prince Ed. Id. { set of 1860—2d, 3d., 4d., 4½d.,6d.,and 9d. } 1 00
                { " 1872—1c., 2c., 3c., 4c., 6c.,and 12c. }
Honduras Republic 1877, prov'l—2r., green surch'ged 2r.,
  1r., black... 75
Honduras Republic, 1877, prov'l—2r., rose, surch'ged 2r.,
  blue... 1 00
Stamps marked * are used.

Return postage must accompany enquiries.

Choice consignments of *rarities only* sent on approval to
parties making deposit.

My approval sheets are the fines in the market. Commission 25%.

The Philatelic Courier

is published quarterly and, as it circulates in all parts of the
world, it is a first-class advertising medium. Subscription
81 per annum. Advertising rates 40 cents per inch. A
moderate rebate made to parties taking larger space or con-
tracting for continued advertisements.

HENRY HECHLER,

Wholesale and retail dealer in

Stamps, Coins and Curiosities,

184 and 185 Argyle St.,

HALIFAX,

NOVA SCOTIA, CANADA.

HERE'S YOUR CHANCE!

FINE Approval Sheets sent on receipt of stamp and A.I.
    ref- 30% Commission allowed. Those remitting $5.00
before August 1st will receive a fine rubber stamp.

E. COLEMAN, C.P.A., 90.

Box 1366   PORTSMOUTH, N.H.

When answering Advertisements please mention this
paper.

CHEAP SETS.

UNUSED.

*12 var. Mexico Post de Mar, 1976	$2 35	
* 5 " Mauritius, Brit	.73	
*7 " Hamburg Envelopes	.05	
10 " Sardinia, 1 and 2c. black, Newspaper incl'd,	.08	
*4 " Hanover S adt post, rare	.08	
24 " German Locals, many rare	.33	
* 5 " Corea, 48	3 var. Corea ...	.30	
*6 " Bavaria Return Letter	.05	

USED AND UNUSED.

15 " U., Locals, genuine...	.25	
20 " " rare,	.40	
25 " " "	.60	

USED.

20 " Bolivar, 1879-85, rare...	1.50	
4 " B. & O, Tel., 1886...	.09	
15 " Egypt, many rare...	.28	
5 " India Service	.15	
* 8 " Italy Pvov., 2c.	.06	
25 " France, 30, 40, 75 and 1f...	.12	
7 " Dutch Indies,...	.12	

* Indicates a comple set. All orders under 50 cents, post-
a'e 5c. extra. Satisfaction guaranteed. All Guaranteed
Genuine.

DIME packets A. & B. contain 120 all different, Japan,
        Cape Good Hope, India and Sweden officials,
Spain, old, new, and war, many kinds, Sardinia, Jamaica,
French Colonies, Australia, Chili Dutch Indies, Ceylon,
Porto Rico, and many other as good, 18c. A positive bargain.
Orders filled by return mail. Give us a trial.

FRANKFORD STAMP COMPANY.

FRANKFORD,   PHILA. PA.

Just published, handsomely bound in gilt cloth, the
Eleventh Edition of

THE IMPROVED POSTAGE STAMP ALBUM.

Revised and corrected to 1887. This album is the most complete, the cheapest, and the largest published at the price.
None can compare with it as to quality of paper, quantity of
pages (no less than 256), and general arrangement. Price
3s. 6d., post free.

NEW AND IMPROVED PACKETS.

TWELVE UNUSED VARIETIES.—Siam, Bosnia, Brazil, 1885,
Porto Rico, Monaco, Roman States, Cyprus, 2½d., Servia,
Mauritius, etc. Post free, 7d.

TWENTY UNUSED VARIETIES.—1d. Cyprus, Czernawodo,
Gibraltar, Portuguese Indies, Bhopal, Japan Envelope, and
others equally rare. ost free, 1s. 1d.

FIFTY USED VARIETIES.—Egypt, Roumelia, Chili, Levant,
Greece, Java, etc. Post free, 7d.

FIFTY USED VARIETIES.—Daccan, Bulgaria, Portuguese
Indies, Sandwich Isles, Finland, Argentine, etc. Post free,
1s. 1d.

Full particulars of all the above, and hundreds of other
Sets and Packets, are given in the new 1887 ILLUSTRAT-
ED FOREIGN STAMP AND CREST PROSPECTUS,
crown 4to. 12 pages, containing a variety of information
valuable to Collectors. Sent to any address, post free, on
application.

STANLEY GIBBONS, & Co., 8, Gower St., London, W.C.

COLLECTORS

desiring rare stamps on approval will please write me. Reference required.
    32 pp. Illustrrted Catalogue for stamp.

W. F. GREANY,

827 Brennan St.   San Francisco, Cal.

MARCH 1888.

Toronto
Philatelic Journal

A Monthly Magazine For Stamp Collectors

NORTH AMERICA

SOUTH AMERICA

TORONTO PHILATELIC CO
106 HURON STREET.

TORONTO CANADA.

Toronto Philatelic Journal.

OFFICIAL ORGAN OF CANADIAN PHILATELIC ASSOCIATION

VOL. 2   TORONTO, MARCH, 1888.   No. 9.

MACAO.

BY HENRY HECHLER.

The last provisional issue of Macao, which appeared in the fall of 1887, are quite interesting to students of philately, being entirely unique, as regards their different details.

The previous provisionals were a series of postal stamps of the face values of 80,100 and 200 reis, which were sur-charged with lower values and served for a time. When the supply of these became exhausted and the new stock that had been ordered from the home govern-ment not arriving they resorted to using the fiscals—the "Imposto do Sellos"—which are 1¾ inches in length and 1 1/16 inches in width. The values thus ap-propriated for postal purposes were the 10, 20 and 60 reis. The base color of the stamps is green. A frame work ⅛ inches wide runs round the outer margin of the stamps. The centre of the stamp is occupied by the Portuguese coat of arms surrounded by an oval band. The ground work between the coat of arms and the band being filled in with fine horizontal lines of yellow. The ground of the band is green with a narrow white line inside and another outside of it. The upper semi-oval bears in white capital letters the inscription : "IMPOSTO DO

SELLOS," and in the lower in the same letters the word "MACAN." On either side between the upper and the lower inscriptions are three small rosettes with a star between each. A rectangular frame immediately surrounds the oval band, leaving a triangular space at each corner, which is filled in with scroll work. This frame measures 1 1/16 inches by 13/16 inch. Thus between this frame and the outer one spoken of above a space remains at the top and at the bottom of the stamp of ¼ inches in depth, inner measurement. This is made into a pan-nel which is filled with fine yellow, per-pendicular but broken lines. The upper pannel bears in black figures the original fiscal value with an oblong rosette on either side of the figures. The lower pannel has in large black capitals the word "REIS" and an ornamental lance —head shape from the outer border of the pannel pointing inwards. The outer frame is traversed by fine lines ; those across the top and bottom being per-pendicular, and those on the sides run-ning horizontally. The small squares thus formed at each corner bear a rosette each. In preparing these fiscal stamps to be used for postal purposes perfora-tion lines were run across, above and below so as to divide the pannels above described from the body of the stamp

and other perforation lines dividing off
the outer frame work on the sides.
They were then surcharged in vermillion
in three lines—in the centre of the coat
of arms was the new figure of value in a
large block letter ; directly above the
coat of arms the word " CORREO," and
below in heavier but somewhat smaller
type the word " REIS." The new values
thus surcharged were 5, 10, and 40 reis.
In the 10 r. the word " CORREO " is
printed in smaller type than in the other
surcharges. The five surcharge is found
on the 10, 20 and 60 reis of which the
first-named are the rarest as only a small
number were issued. Moderate number
of the 20's were surcharged and they are
esteemed almost as highly as the 10's
There were more of the 60's so surcharged than any other and they are therefore not so rare. The 10 was surcharged
on the 10 and the 40 on the 20 reis
fiscal

It was optional with the public in
using them to place them on the letters
or parcels either entire or to tear away
the portions perforated off if room was
needed. Of course those used entire are
regarded as far more valuable, com-
manding three times as much as those
which were curtailed.

My object in writing this short sketch
is to advise philatelic friends, if these
stamps come into their hands, to preserve
them entire.

This provisional series was in use for
a very short time, only when the new
series—which is similar to the new
ssamps of Portugal and its colonies, and
bears the portrait of the king in relief—
were received and went into immediate
use. Therefore these provisionals must
become extremely valuable before long.

The values and colors of the new
series are as follows :

5 reis black.	50 reis blue.
10 " green.	80 " slate.
20 " carmin.	100 " red-brawn
25 " violet.	200 " lilac.
40 " brown.	300 " orange.

The crown type series thus becomes
obsolete.

CORRESPONDENCE.

Letters of enquiry not accompanied by 3c. for postage will
be inserted under this heading.

J. A. P., Hamilton.—The Philatelic
Courier was not the first stamp paper published in Canada. In 1865 Mr. George
Stewart, of St. Johns, N.B., published the
Stamp Collector's Monthly journal. In
1868, Mr. Scott, a clerk in the law firm of
Crooks, Kingsmill & Catanach, published
the Stamp Advocate in this city; and in
1874 two stamp papers were published—
the Collector and the Beaver. The only
catalogues of revenue stamps published in
Canada to our knowledge was that of
Gibson & Co. in 1875, that of Mr. F.
H. Best in 1877 and Mr. Ketchesn's,
1887.

J. H. R., Montreal.—Neither stamps
nor envelopes are of any philatelic value,
any one may register a letter with ordinary
postage stamps.

A. H. W., Toronto.—The rubber stamp
impressions of Jays Despatch which you
refer to, and which have also been mentioned in some of the leading American
philatelic papers, are of no philatelic value
whatever. It is only a scheme of young
Jay's, a stamp collector of La Hoyt,
Iowa., seeking for notriety.

H. A. N., N. Y.—Halifax was not the
first to organize a philatelic society.
Toronto had a philatelic society in 1885.

A. B. B., Syracuse—Stamps imported
into Canada, whether used or unused, are
classed as engraved paper, on which a
duty of 30% is imposed.

For the TORONTO PHILATELIC JOURNAL.

Pithy Philatelic Pointers.

BY CANADENSIS

I have at last succeeded in unearthing something novel. A person high in official position in 1882 was ordered to burn all the remaining bill stamps of the Government. In handling over a number of sheets of the third issue $3 stamps, he came across a sheet of the same *unperforated* and *ungummed*. Permission was given for the official to retain some of them, and for a long time they were lost to his knowledge. In looking over some old envelopes the other day he came across two unsevered and these are now in the possession of Mr. J. R. Hooper, who refused a fine offer for them.

Speaking of bill stamps reminds me of that useful little catalogue of President Ketcheson's. I hope he will give us the price both for *used* and *unused* specimens, as the latter are decidedly the best and rarest of the bills, and U S. collectors are beginning to enquire largely after them.

The C.P.A. Exchange Department, I see, is now in good running order, and Mr. Grenny deserves great credit for his system of working this important office.

I would like to see all the officers send in their reports monthly to the official organ.

Where will the C P.A. Convention be held at next election ? Toronto or Montreal would seem fitting places

I hope every one will send all their old catalogues and papers, etc., to our Librarian, Mr. Walker. By the way, I see the latter gentleman was in Ottawa with Mr. Hooper last week. Walker is a dandy curler, and belongs to the champion team which won the Governor-General's cup.

Let all C.P.A. members use Scott's catalogue as a standard, and when Ketcheson's new list for British North America comes out it will be the standard for Canada.

I see there is talk in the U.S. of the dealers using the A.P.A. exchange dept. to sell their stamps. I am sure our C.P.A. executive and officers will shut down if anything is attempted here. How would a limit on sheets do ?

Can any of our collectors inform us of the following firms, stamps being sent to them and no reply received after writing three times in each case :—Max Richter, Chemintz, Saxony ; Jas. Steiner, Honolulu, Hawaii ; T. B. Meyer, Callas, Peru ; Edw. Heim, Vienna, Austria ; Benjamin & Bannister, London, Eng. Any word whether these parties are alive or not will benefit philately.

Yours philatelically

CANADENSIS.

Philatelic Tid-Bits.

BY HENRY S. HARTE.

The first stamp paper published is the United States appeared in 1867. F. Triffet, Boston, Mass., was the publisher.

During 1887 there were published six papers in Canada devoted wholly or partially to the interests of philatelists.

Dr. Stephan, a German State official, is said to be the originator of the Post Card. Autria was the first country however to use them ; its first issue was Oct., 1869 ; Hungary Nov. 1st, 1869, and Germany not until July, 1870.

Japan has the cheapest postal service in the world.

Monsieur Dr. Velayer, a Frenchman, is said to have used a label or stamp in 1653 as a means of preparing postage on a letter.

A post office was instituted in Paris, France, in 1759. It was a private and not a Government office.

TORONTO
PHILATELIC JOURNAL.

Published on the 1st of every month.

Geo. A. Lowe,   **Jos. Hooper,**
ED. PHILATELIC DEPT.   ED. NUMISMATIC DEPT

SUBSCRIPTION :

United States and Canada 35c. per year; Foreign Countries,
50c. per year.

Advertising Rates :

1 inch..	0 50
2 "	0 80
½ column	1 50
1 "	2 50
1 page..	4 50

10 per cent. discount on standing advts.
Copy wanted not later than the 25th.
Remit money by P.O. order, or small amounts in one or two cent stamps.

Address all correspondence to the

Toronto Philatelic Co.

106 Huron St.   **Toronto, Canada.**

TORONTO, MARCH, 1888.

OWING to lack of space we have been obliged to omit our portrait this month. Our next month's issue will contain that of Mr. F. J. Grenny.

THIS month we had intended to combine the *Niagara Falls Philatelist* and issue a double number, but learning that there was a hitch in the above company we decided to have no connection with it, so we again appear in our old form.

IN the C.P.A. Roll of Members, published in our last issue, No. 57 should read Fred. Burnett instead of T. Burnett, and No. 107, C. A. Townsend, Akron, Ohio, instead of Arkon.

AN error in our last number made the Secretary's report read " I will personally reduce this to *me.*" The latter word should have been *nil.* Quite a difference.

"THE BLUFTON STAMP SOCIETY," by " Philo " is to hand with its 70 pages of interesting matter. Young collectors will find this book very instructive.

THE address of Geo. H. Cox has been changed from 9 Dresden Row, Halifax, to Shelbourne, N.S.

—MR. FRENCH informs us that sickness was the cause of the delay in publishing the *Canadian Philatelist.*

PERU intends to burn a certain proportion of her surplus paper currency monthly until the circulation is reduced to trade requirements.

THE people of Manitoba sent over 4,000,000 letters and postcards through the mails last year. There was an average of 21¼ to each person.

A POSTAGE STAMP EXCHANGE and Mart is shortly to be opened in Vienna. The Austrian Postoffice sells annually 8,000 florins' worth of stamps out of use to collectors. No less than 60,000 florins' worth of Eastern postage stamps are exported every year from Vienna. Cards of admission to the Postage Stamp Exchange will on no conditions be delivered to collectors under 18 years of age.

Its English You Know.

Mr J. A. Caron, formerly of St. Luce Station, Que., informs us that on Feb. 11th, 1887, he sent a post office order to the value of $7.00 to L. D. & J. K. Ferguson, Stamp Dealers of London, England, for 50,00 Continentals. Having written them several times and received no reply he wrote to the Postmaster-General, and received the following reply which speaks for itself:

POST OFFICE DEPARTMENT,
OTTAWA, 22nd Feb., 1888.

Dear Sir,—With further reference to the above noted Money Order, and to the letter from this Branch of 17th ultimo, I beg to say that information has to-day been received from the British Postal Department that payment was made at Vere St. West London Post Office, on 26th February, 1887, to the signature of L. D. & J. K. Ferguson & Co. It is therefore impossible for the amount to be repaid to you.

I am, Dear Sir,
Your obedient servant,
W. J. BARRETT,
for Supt.
J. A. Caron, Esq.,
331 West Superior St.,
Duluth Minn., U.S.

PURCHASING DEPARTMENT OF THE C.P.A.

E. Y. PARKER, AGENT.,
47 HURON STREET.,
TORONTO, CANADA.

This office shall be conducted under the following instructions:

I shall make arrangements to obtain, at as little expense to members as possible, unused specimens of all newly issued stamps, envelopes, postcards, etc., and shall notify members from time to time in the official organ from what countries I am preparing to obtain specimens. I shall not be asked to furnish specimens from any country not so named by me, or to furnish any obsolete, uncurrent, or cancelled specimens (except members wishing to pay current prices for any such stamps they may want, will do my best to secure them) or to supply any member with more than five specimens of the same kind once supplied to the same member, or to supply less than $1.00 (one dollar's)

worth of stamps at one time. Every member desiring to avail himself of the opportunities of this department must deposit in advance with me a sufficient amount to cover the cost of purchases, including all postages and expenses, and in addition a commission of 10% on the amount to be charged by the Purchasing Agent one-half of which I shall hand over to the Treasurer at the close of the fiscal year.

I shall also arrange, as far as practicable, to obtain for such members as shall elect to deposit with me in advance the sum of five dollars ($5) each for that purpose, one specimen, or, if desired, any number not to exceed five of every newly issued stamp, envelope and post card issued, and to distribute the same as soon as received until the amount of each deposit shall be exhausted. Each member contributing to this department may, at the time of making his deposit, specify from what country he desires newly issued stamps, or may limit his request to stamps of not more than a certain value, and may renew or increase his deposit from time to time as the same is diminished. Stamps distributed in this manner shall be charged against the deposit at the same rate as before provided, including postage, expenses and commission.

I shall receive and publish in the official organ lists of varieties which may be desired by members of the Association. I shall receive and publish in the official organ lists of such rarities as members of the Association may send from time to time for sale. Members sending in such stamps, etc., must state price they ask for each, and the specimens so advertised shall be sold to the first person applying therefor.

All stamps so sent to me shall be accompanied by a sum sufficient to pay the postage and registration fee for the return of the stamps or remittances, and every application for a stamp or stamps so advertised must be accompanied by the amount by the amount necessary to pay the postage and registration fee, in addition to the price, in cash, check, or money order.

All stamps, etc., sent in for sale, shall be held for thirty days after the appearance of the official journal announcing the offer of the same, and if not then disposed of shall be returned to the owner. The Purchasing Agent shall deduct 5 per cent. from the price realized for every stamp when remitting to the owner for the same.

The Purchasing Agent shall give bond to the Trustees in the sum of one hundred dollars.

THE C.P.A.

PRESIDENT'S REPORT.

To the Members of the C.P.A.:

GENTLEMEN,—As our Association is now thoroughly organized and election over, I have to thank you for the confidence you have reposed in me by electing me as your first President.

I can assure you that I will do all in my power to advance the interests of our Association, and feel confident that every member will do the same.

The Exchange Superintendent has shown a good deal of enterprise and energy in getting his department in working order so soon, and I trust all the members will avail themselves of this opportunity to exchange their duplicates, and thus increase their collections at a very small cost to themselves; be sure and order a supply of sheets, fill them up and return to the Superintendent at once.

The Librarian will be pleased to receive all the philatelic literature you can send him, and I hope every member will contribute something.

It will be the duty of the Executive Committee to fill the vacancies for Counterfeit Detector and Purchasing Agent as soon as possible so that the members can avail themselves of the benefit to be derived from this department.

Yours sincerely,
H. F. KETCHESON, *President.*

SECRETARY'S REPORT.

To the Members of the C.P.A.:

GENTLEMEN,—It gives me much pleasure to present you with my first report of the progress of our society for the past month. Our success is now assured. At the time of writing the membership numbers 110. Two of our members, Nos. 65 and 102, have resigned. I must say that I have not been burdened with many dues. Members will please take notice that April 8th is the limit of time for payment of dues, and also that all dues are payable not to the Treasurer but to me. Membership cards will be issued as soon as possible and will be sent to all members paying their dues. The offices of Counterfeit Detector and Vice Presidents for B.C. and Manitoba are yet unfilled, but appointments will be made before my next report is presented. The constitution will also be issued in the near future. I beg to inform the members that note-heads bearing the official imprint can be had from me at the following prices—per 250, $1.25; per 500, $2.00. Officers will please communicate with me stating how many note-heads they desire and their wants will be promptly attended to. Following are the lists of new members and applicants:

NEW MEMBERS LIST, NO. I.

109—David A. Waton, Box 294, Dundas, Ont.
110—M. Brill, 28 Sutton Place, New York.
111.—H. A. Babb, Box 3081, Denver, Col
112—J. C. Feldwisch, Box 2022, Denver, Col.

APPLICATIONS FOR MEMBERSHIP.

H. R. Donohue, 16 Cliff St., St. John, N.B. Reference, Henry S. Harte.

Percival Parrish, 53 Washington St., Providence, R.I. A.P.A. member. Reference, none given.

W. H. Bacon, West Newton, Mass. A.P.A. 339. Reference, none given.

C. B. Russell, 205 Main St., Marlboro, Mass. Reference, none given.

The name of V. Gurdji, No. 101, Galveston, Texas, was given by misprint last month as V. Gurd, Jr.

Blank applications for membership and lull particulars can be obtained by addressing me.

J. A. LEIGHTON, Secy.

LIBRARIAN'S REPORT.

To the Members of the C.P.A.

GENTLEMEN, —As I have been elected to the office of Librarian of the Canadian Philatelic Association, I desire to acknowledge the receipt of donations received as follows :

Mr. H F. Ketcheson, 32 pieces, including his catalogue of Canadian stamps.

Mr. S. M. Wolsieffer, copies of Philatelical Waltzes, Postal Card Galops and Good-By Old Stamps, Good By.

Mr. Walker, 27 pieces, and from the Western Philatelic Publishing Co. complete file of the Western Philatelist.

I am especially indebted to Mr. S. B. Bradt for a copy of his book " The Bluffton Stamp Society," a file each of the Collectors' Companion, Stamp Collector, Philatelic Magazine, Durbins Standard Catalogue, Sixteenth Edition, and 5 pieces, and to Mr. H. L. Hart for bound copy of Vol. I., Halifax Philatelist.

I have received the current numbers of TORONTO PHILATELIC JOURNAL, Western Philatelist and Halifax Philatelist.

It has been suggested that we make a collection of photographs of members of the Association. I would earnestly request the members to forward their photographs to the library as early as convenient.

I hope the members will continue to take an interest in the library and make the receipts for the coming month exceed that of the past.

GEORGE WALKER, Librarian.

Peterboro', March 9th, 1888.

To Members C.P.A.

GENTLEMEN,— Mr. E. Y. Parker having received a plurality of votes both as Official Editor and Purchasing Agent, has resigned the former office in favor of Mr. George A. Lowe, Editor of the *Toronto Philatelic Journal.* Therefore, in order to avoid further delay we hereby declare the said E. Y. Parker as being elected to fill the office of Purchasing Agent, and the said Geo. A. Lowe that of Official Editor.

J. A. LEIGHTON,
J. REGINALD HOOPER,
F. J. GRENNY,
Committee on Election C.P.A.

NUMISMATIC DEPARTMENT.

All correspondence in this Department should be addressed to Joseph Hooper, Box 145 Port Hope.

The Sarcophagus of " Alexander the Great " has been discovered at Saida.

A Silver Medal is to hand of Montreal Jesuits' College. Militia of the Pope, with red ribon. Obverse : bust of Virgin Mary. Reverse : Our Saviour. Size : 12 M.

Twenty-seven die varieties of St. Ann de Beaupre Medals have so far come to our knowledge. In metal and die varieties we number twenty-nine.

The Dominion Exhibition Medal of September, 1880, occurs with and without Lymburgner in the field. The name in field is claimed as a rarity.

The 1887 10c. piece has turned up. This will make so far as known for this year three issues—10c., 5c., 1c.

The largest collection of coins, 125,000 in number, is in the cabinet of antiquities, Vienna. 50,000 are Greek and Roman.

It is said that in the southern part of Russia the peasants use a coin of such small value that if would take 250,000 of them to buy a Canadian dollar, and these coins are so scarce that a man who has a hundred is looked upon as rich, and one who has a thousand is considered very wealthy. It is strange to think a person wealthy who owns two-fifths of a cent, and comfortably well off on one-twenty-fifths of a cent.

A coin is said to be "*proof*" when it is specially struck by hand press, instead of by steam press, from a polished planchet, and a "*proof set*" is a complete set of proofs of current coins. A "*pattern piece*" is an early specimen of proof from a newly adopted coinage die or dies. An impression in soft metal to test an experimental die is called a "*trial piece.*" When a piece is struck from regular dies on experimental dies with experimental legends, devices or designs, it is denominated an "*experimental piece.*" Trial and experimental pieces, struck for mint purposes only, will not be issued, circulated or sold. Pieces popularly known as restrikes, false metal pieces and metallic replicas, or copies, are prohibited by the revised U.S. statutes. Proof and pattern pieces are sold by the superintendent of the U.S. mint. The superintendent will furnish, without charge, a pattern piece to any incorporated numismatic society in the United States. In such cases, if the pattern be in gold or silver, the value of the metal will be required.

A Buffalo milkman wears a nickel five-cent piece as a watch charm, and gives this reason : " Over five years ago I took this nickel, which was then beautifully gold plated, as a $5 gold piece, in payment of a bill. As soon as I detected the fraud I took it back to the woman who passed it on me, but she refused to make it good. So I fastened it to my watch chain and kept on supplying her with milk, But now every day I make her quart one-fourth water; and once a week I credit her with one-fourth the amount of her milk bill. When the sum total standing to her credit is $4.95 she shall have pure milk once more, and not until then. She knows the milk is watered, but whenever she shows an inclination to complain, I handle the nickle and say that my milk is as "pure as gold." That settles it.

Col Bacon, Secretary of the Dominion Rifle Association, has written to Messrs. Elkington, of London, England, who have up to the present time been the manufacturers of the D.R.A. medals, asking them to forward the dies in their possession, as the medals will in future be produced in Canada. The expenditure for medals has amounted to from two to three hundred dollars yearly, and by this step the D.R.A. will save about $50 per annum, or in fact about $1 on each medal, as on an average 50 medals are manufactured every year. At the council meeting of the D.R.A. a day or two ago, specimens of medals were supplied from Montreal and Toronto manufacturers. It is the intention of the D.R.A. to ask for tenders, as soon as the dies are received, for the manufacture of the medals for 1833. It is probable that either Montreal or Toronto will get order.

The Editor of this Department, while in Montreal lately, spent a pleasant and agreeable time among the leading numismatists of that city, the guest of R. W. McLachlan, Esq., author of " Canadian Numismatics;" a very pleasant evening was spent at the Antiquarian Society's monthly meetings. An introduction to the various members of the society, the pleasure of listening to an able paper by Mr. H. Mott, The medal ordered by the society in Berlin (to commemorate the 25th anniversary of the foundation of the society) has not given satisfaction to the larger portion of the members, the " early Italian style" being copied by the artist who was entrusted with its execution. The spirit and intention of the designer to represent the " Antique," does not agree with a majority of the members' ideas as to their requirement. A "Jeton" also has been struck in connection with the anniversary in the same style of art. A further description of the above will be given when the medals (to which we have subscribed) are received.

APRIL 1888.

Toronto
Philatelic Journal

A Monthly Magazine For Stamp Collectors

TORONTO PHILATELIC CO
106 HURON STREET.

TORONTO CANADA.

TOR. ENG. CO.

Toronto Philatelic Journal.

OFFICIAL ORGAN OF CANADIAN PHILATELIC ASSOCIATION

| Vol. 2 | TORONTO, APRIL, 1888. | No. 10. |

OUR CANADIAN PHILATELISTS.

F. J. GRENNY.

This is the third portrait in our series of Canadian. Philatelists: appearing in uniform, and it is noticeable that quite a number of men of stamp have military affinities. for instance, Major Evans and Lt. Partello, in the front rank of Philately. Our American cousins will begin to think the C.P.A. is made up of colors, etc. The subject of our sketch was born in Brantford, Ontario, in 1840, and has been engaged in Post Office work since 1852. When in St. George P.O. and in charge of Morrisburg P.O. from 1855 to 1858, he sold large numbers of the old pence issues of Canada postage stamps at face value to the public, and is now regretting the lost opportunity. At that time no idea of stamp collecting was entertained by him, or possibly by any one else in Canada. Since 1870 he has been employed in the Brantford P.O., and has bandled and delivered millions of stamps, letters, etc., there. As an instance of the large increase in postal business still going on Mr. Grenny says the sale of stamps in the Brantford P.O. for three months in 1870 was about $500. and now the amount sold is about $25,000 per annum. He began his first collection from seeing a small album of stamps owned by a student. This collection he sold to Mr Grenslade, then of Toronto. His present collection is not very large (about 4,000 varieties) but is choice, being largely composed of picked specimens a number of varieties and a few oddities. He aims to have a complete collection of all the stamps of our own country, and has about 100 varieties of Canada postage stamps, cards and wrappers. These include varieties in shade, etc., also a complete set of proofs of Canada postage stamps. Does not use an album or book, the specimens all being mounted on prepared cardboard. His collection of about 600 varieties of Canadian coins and medals is also very fine and interesting. Among other varieties we noticed " Fishery Rights for N. F.," White Farthing Leslie 2d. Brit. Settlement, K., etc Mr. Grenny has been a member of the active militia since 1854, took part in the 1866 campaign, and holds the rank of Major in the Dufferin Rifles of Canada, is a charter member of the C.P.A.,and was recently elected Exchange Superintendent of the C.P.A. He has about 150 complete volumes (a few bound) of philatelic periodicals all English, American and Canadian.

—The 5c. register will become more scarce now that the fee to the U.S. is only 2 cents.

—We have received the 3c. Canadian stamp with W. I. S. perforated across the face.

—The 10c. Canadian is now changed to a dark rose color.

THE C.P.A.

SECRETARY'S REPORT.

To the Members of the C.P.A.:

GENTLEMEN,—Our society is growing steadily and surely. We close the month with 114 members and 5 applications on hand. By a typographical error last month, Mr. David Watson's name appeared as Waton. My intimation that the dues should be paid forthwith seems to have had little effect, as but few members have settled their accounts. I shall notify all delinquents immediately and the names of such as fail to settle their accounts previous to May o will be published in the May number. The names of those on whom this fails to produce any effect will be removed from our membership rolls. Membership cards have been issued and will be sent to all paying their dues. The following appointments have been made—Counterfeit Detector, A. B S. DeWolfe, Halfax, N.S; Vice- President for Manitoba, J. R. Davidson, Brandon ; Vice-President for British Columbia and the N. W. Territories, J. H. Todd, Hector, B. C. All the above gentlemen have the interests of the Association at heart, and will perform their duties to the satisfaction of the entire Society. I beg to quote the following prices for note-heads : per 150,$1 ; 250, $1.25; per 500, $2.00; per 1,000, $3.50. Samples can now be had on application to me. Below will be found the list of new members and applicants :

LIST OF NEW MEMBERS, NO. 2.

113—H. R. Donohoe, 16 Cliff St., St. John, N.B.

114—Percival Parrish, 53 Washington St., Newport, R.I. (given by mistake last month as Providence, R.I.)

115—W. H. Bacon, West Newton, Mass.

116—C. B. Russell, 205 Main St., Marlboro', Mass.

LIST OF APPLICATION, NO. 2.

John S. Bixby, 835 West Main St., Decatur, Ill. Reference, A.P.A.

Maurice E. Finney, Harrisburg, Pa. Reference, Dr. Geo. W. Reily, Pres. Harrisburg National Bank ; J. Uhler, Cashier Harrisburg National Bank.

Cleo. C. Morency, Box 573, Quebec City. References, H. F. Ketcheson ; J. B. Moens.

Walter D. Morton, care of Dr. Morton, Barrie, Ont. References, E. D. Morton, M.D.; Will. D. B. Spry.

Fr. Gottorf, cor. York and Caroline Sts., Hamilton, Ont. References, J. R. Hooper, Mrs. Wallace Mason.

J. A. LEIGHTON,
Orangeville, Ont., Apr. 9th, 1888.

LIBRARIAN'S REPORT.

I am glad to report that the members continue to take an interest in the Association Library, as evinced by the receipts for the past month.

Donations were received as follows :

Mr. Geo. A. Lowe, Vol. I. of TORONTO PHILATELIC JOURNAL bound in cloth.

Mr. J. A. Leighton, 52 pieces ; J. R. Hooper, Scott's Catalogue, 49 edition and 7 pieces. Mr. Patrick Chalmers, 2 pieces ; E. O. Evans, 2 pieces, and from F. E. Book, complete file of the Niagara Falls Philatelist. I have received current numbers of the TORONTO PHILATELIC JOURNAL, the Western Philatelist, the Curiosity World, Plain Talk, the Hawkeye State Collector, the Stamp, the Eastern Philatelist, the Charleston Philatelist. From the authors I have received R. R. Bogert & Co.'s Standard Catalogue, copies of the Stamp Dealers of the United States, by H. A. Babb, and W. P. Brown's Catalogue No. 7.

I have received photographs of Major H. Hechler, H. F. Ketcheson and Geo. Walker. I hope that all members of the Association will send at least one piece as a donation to the library during the coming month, and as many as can make it convenient to send their phof.

GEO. WALKER, Librarian,
Peterboro', April 10, 1888.

REPORT OF EXCHANGE SUPERINTENDENT.

In addition to the circular sent to all members last month containing Rules and Regulations in full, further instructions for the management of this Department of the C.P.A. are published in this issue of the TORONTO PHILATELIC JOURNAL. They are very plain, so that every member can participate in the benefits to be derived from sending their stamps on circuit, and receiving others to select from. The stamps should be marked at cash prices and as low as possible. This will ensure good exchanges or sales They will be charged at prices marked to the members who retain them, their own sheets being on circuit at same time, the amount taken from their sheets will l e credited to them and the balance drawn. The superintendent will render quarterly statements, and the balance if in favor of Department must be paid to him in cash. The price charged for sheets and covers is to defray the necessary expenses of the Department. I have received to 10th of April 128 filled sheets and covers, values nearly $500, and sent out 300 blank sheets and covers. All the exchange books are now circulating among the members in the exchange. I am much pleased to announce that the Halifax Philatelic Society has become a branch of the Exchange Department, with Mr. Frank C. Kaye, of the Halifax Postoffice, as manager. Their membership is over 20. I would again ask those members who have not yet sent in exchange sheers, etc., to do so at once. The more members avail themselves of the benefits of the Exchange Department the greater will be the individual benefit and success of the Exchange. The stamps should be marked at least 25% below Scott's last catalogue.

F. J. GRENNY, Supt. Ex. Dept. C.P.A.

TORONTO
PHILATELIC JOURNAL.

Published on the 1st of every month.

Ceo. A. Lowe,   **Jos. Hooper,**
ED. PHILATELIC DEPT.   ED. NUMISMATIC DEPT.

SUBSCRIPTION :

United States and Canada 35c. per year; Foreign Countries,
50c. per year.

Advertising Rates :

1 inch...	0 50
2 "	0 80
½ column	1 50
1 "	2 50
1 page...	4 50

10 per cent. discount on standing advts.
Copy wanted not later than the 25th.
Remit money by P.O. order, or small amounts in one or
two cent stamps.
Address all correspondence to the

Toronto Philatelic Co.
106 Huron St.   **Toronto, Canada.**

TORONTO, APRIL, 1888.

WE have received from Mr. Babb a
copy of "The Stamp Dealers of the
United States." A directory which contains the names and addresses of the
leading dealers of the United States.

MESSRS. STANLEY, GIBBONS & CO.,
have forwarded us the second supplement of the Philatelic Handbook, by
Major Evans. It contains all the postal
issues of 1886 and 1887. This is a valuable work and should be in the library
of every philatelist.

CAN any of our readers give us any
information concerning the following
parties: Frank S. Perry, Box 255, Yarmouth, Maine; R. Vansyekel, Box 604
and 2438, Bridgeton, N.Y.

CORRESPONDENCE.

*Letters of enquiry not accompanied by 3c. for postage will
be inserted under this heading.*

A. E. Smith, Halifax.—T. P. J. was
forwarded to you on Feb. 20th. As a
rule we take no notice of postals

W. H. B.—We know nothing of Gre-
gory, of Hamilton.

F. J. G —We expect to publish a
catalogue of Canadian postage and
revenue some time next fall.

For the Toronto Philatelic Journal

POSTAGE STAMPS AS A PAS-
TIME.

BY MRS J. A. MASON.

The practice of collecting postage
stamps is now universally acknowledged
to be one of the most useful and elevat-
ing of all pastimes. True, many raise
the objection that it is so expensive.
But what pastime is there that is not
attended with some outlay, and judging
by comparison stamps rank about the
cheapest.

Many a successful business man to-
day dates his first business venture back
to the time when he bought a packet of
thirty stamps for a nickel and sold them
at a cent apiece, realizing what he considered a small fortune of profit in the
transaction.

A poor man living in Denmark had
adquired a love of Philately when a
small boy, saving every cent to add to
his collection. Born of lowly parents
and having to work very hard, his education was necessarily very limited, but by
his constant devotion to his favorite
amusement he became familiar with the
various countries and their rulers, and
naturally of an investigating turn of

mind he became interested in reading about those couutries represented on his stamps. On arriving at maturity he had acquired a good general knowledge of history, as well as geography. With this knowledge also came the desire to travel and visit other countries and perhaps gratify the craving of ambition by becoming a wealthy man. But how to attain this object with his meagre income was a question. Finally he decided to visit Copenhagen and arrange for the sale of his collection which numbered between five and six thousand. He was so successful that he realized sufficient to enable him to visit the Uuited States and Canada. Now he is a prosperous tradesman on the fair way to fortune, rapidly realizing all his boyish day-dreams of success. Another case came under my observation. A young man came from England to reside in Canada, bringing with him a very fine collection of stamps. He secured work in one of our large cities, and for a while all went well, but depression in trade, followed by the failing of his employer, threw him out of a situation just in the beginning of the dull season.

Having no friends and few resources, his money soon spent, no opportunity afforded for replenishing his exchequer till he bethought him of his collection. When to his satisfaction he sold it for sufficient to tide him over his difficulties. Such are some of the advantages accruing from money carefully invested.

Exchange Department C.P.A.

1. The object of this Exchange Department of this Association is to facilitate the exchange of duplicate stamps. entire envelopes and postal cards, among its members. This end will be attained by the use of exchange books and boxes, as provided in the Appendix, which is annexed hereto.

2 To simplify the workings of the Exchange, Article VIII, of the Constitution provides for the formation of Branch Societies in places where six or more members of the Association can be brought together, or any existing society with the requisite number of members, can be entered as a Branch by applying to the Secretary. By the aid of these branches a number of members deal with the Exchange as one, and the main object of Philatelic societies, the exchange of duplicates, is attained.

3 Individual members not residing where a branch socity is located, are entitled to all the privileges of the Exchange, in the same manner, and under the same conditions as a branch society.

4 The Secretary of each Branch Society must furnish the Superintendent with a list of its officers and members, with full Post Office address of each.

5 In case the Superintendent is prevented by sickness, or other cause, from performing his duties, the Board of Officers may appoint a substitute to act during such incapacity.

6 Branch Societies are allowed, when practicable, to receive as many exchange sheets and envelopes as they send out.

7 Branch Societies are allowed to keep exchange sheets and envelopes three days for each member participating, and three days to make up the account. A fine of ten cents a day is imposed for each day the exchanges are kept over the established time. Branches must decide among themselves the order of preference in choosing from exchanges.

8 When sending exchanges the Superintendent will designate a circuit route, which must be strictly adhered to. At the time of forwarding exchanges to the next member on the circuit, the Superintendent must be notified by postal card. giving date and total of the amount taken by the senders.

9 Branch Societies are responsible for what they have on hand from the day of receipt to the day of sending, and for any difference that may arise during that time. The Superintendent may refuse the privilege of the exchange to any one not settling accounts promptly when rendered.

10 Each Branch must prepay the postage in forwarding exchanges, which must be registered if their value is over ten dollars, or be sent at the risk of the senders.

11 In planning the order of circulation, the Superintendent will use the rule of rotation, in order that each member may have an equal chance in first choice, the party being second in the first exchange being first in the second, and so on.

12 The Superintendent has first choice of all exchanges. He can also send his own sheets free.

12 The Trustees shall decide upon all cases of misunderstanding that may arise in this department.

— —

MANAGEMENT OF EXCHANGE BOOKS AND BOXES.

1. Members wishing to avail themselves of the facilities of this department can obtain the official exchange sheets for adhesive stamps and cut envelopes, and covers for entire envelopes, Postal cards, etc.. of the Superintendent. Five cents each will be charged for these, which must be remitted with the order. They will be sent postpaid.

2. Members must remove the paper from the backs of stamps, and attach them to the sheets with gummed paper hinges, in order that they may be examined for water marks, etc. Space is provided on the sheets for the owner's name, name of the branch society to which he belongs, and the value of the sheet. Each member marks his own prices ; the Superintendent adds the sheet and book numbers.

3. The envelope for entire specimens must not contain more than twenty pieces.

They are printed with space for owner's name, list of contents, price of each, total value, name and circulation number of those who remove specimens, &c. A number in pencil can be placed on each piece to correspond with the list number on the outside of the envelope.

4 Members having prepared their sheets for circulation, will promptly mail them to the Superintendent, who will make them into books and boxes, and place them upon the circuit.

5 Several sheets bound together constitute an exhange book, and a number of envelopes an exchange box.

6. In dealing with Branch Societies the Superintendent will draw balances as a whole for each branch, dealing with its Secretary, who will adjust the account with his members. The Secretary will also gather the sheets of his branch, and mail together in sending them to the Superintendent.

7. After exchanges have completed their circuit, and are returned to the Superintendent, he will render an account to each participant. Eight days are allowed after members receive their statements, in which to settle balances due the exchange department. Balances due to members will be remitted as soon as the accounts can be adjusted.

Philatelic Tid-Bits.

— —

The first U.S. post card was issued May 1st, 1873.

The first list of postage stamps was published by a Mr. Brown of London, England, in 1862.

English mails were first carried by rail in 1830.

A collector of stamps was unknown until about 1854. Stamp dealers were not heard of before 1860.

There are over 200 varieties of Canadian Revenue Stamps.

The first Canadian postage stamps were issued in 1851. Thirty-six varieties have been issued up to date.

The first Canadian post cards were issued in 1877. Nine varieties are known to exist exclusive of varieties in paper and shades in color.

There were fifty two different Philatelic papers issued during the past year, of which eleven ceased to exist before its close.

The Philatelic Monthly is the oldest existing Philatelic paper. It is now in its 14th volume.

The first Post Office in America is said to have been established in Phiadelphia, Pa.

More anon,
HENRY S. HARTE.

New Brunrwick Vice-President's Report.

To the Members of the C.P.A.

GENTLEMEN,—It affords me much pleasure in presenting you with this my first report. My only regret is that it is not a more encouraging one. Philatelists are not to be found at the present moment in such numbers in New Brunswick as in some other parts of the Dominion. The reason of this dearth I am not in a position to account for ; perhaps it may be because Philatelia has not shed her rays of light into the nooks and corners of our Province as fully as she has done elsewhere ; but be it as it may there is sufficiently good material to work upon to tell a different story before many months are passed.

At the end of March I visited St. John (the city by the sea) in the interests of our Association, my visit affording me much encouragement I found that the city could boast of several gentlemen who had been ardent collectors in the days of yore and who possesses to-day collections, which to say the least of, would make the eyes of many of our members water. (The majority of the collections possessed specimens of the Cormell Stamp). I endeavored to awaken in these gentlemen an interest in their old love, so all with with I came in contact I extolled the benefits to be derived from membership in the C.P.A., and I trust that my feeble efforts may be the means not only of adding to our roll of membership several St. John Philatelists, but also that we may soon see a branch of our Association organized in that city.

It is my intention, when time permits, to visit all the different cities of N.B., and I trust that ere the year dies out, our Province will be as well represented upon the C.P.A. roll of membership as any of the other Provinces in the Dominion.

Thanking you, gentlemen, for having given me the honor of being the first New Brunswick Vice-President of the C.P.A.

Yours fraternally,
HENRY S. HARTE.

MAY 1888.

Toronto Philatelic Journal

A Monthly Magazine For Stamp Collectors

CANADA NORTH AMERICA

SOUTH AMERICA

TORONTO PHILATELIC CO
106 HURON STREET.

TORONTO CANADA.

Postoffice Department...	... ...	10	$1.75
Interior "	... ...	10	1.50
War "	... ...	11	.75
Postoffice ...	... ...	4	.25
Locals ...	... ...	7	.12
Telegraph ...	... ...	5	.07

Exchange wanted. Approval sheets for reference.

N. E. CARTER, DELAVAN, WIS., U.S.A.

Please name this paper in answering advertisements.

IMPORTANT NOTICE.

I MUST hereby thank my many friends and patrons for the kind support tendered me in my business during the past few years, which I must say has been beyond my most sanguine expectations.

I regret to announce that Mr. Dill, who has been with me for the past eight months, has been unable to continue in the business on account of sickness in his family, which caused him to give up all business duties.

In the future Mr. Wm. C. Atcheson will manage the stamp business with the aid of Geo. W. Atcheson. Mr. Atcheson is a prominent philatelist and I feel sure that my many patrons will continue their favors, assuring them that all orders will be filled promptly. I remain yours philatelically,

M. D. BATCHELDER.

BATCHELDER'S
MOUND CITY POPULAR PACKETS.

Packet No. 32 contains 1,000 different postage stamps, being a complete collection in itself. This packet contains many rare stamps, among which are, Argentine, 90c. Cape of Good Hope, Triangular, Newfoundland, (Triangular), China, Cuba, Ceylon, rare surcharges.

Ecuador, Mexican—many varieties. Persia Official, United States Newspaper stamps, also obsolete envelopes. State Department, unused and other excellent stamps. We will send this packet post free, and registered for $10.

Packet No. 33 contains 500 different stamps, including Argentine, Azores, Brazil, Bulgaria, Bosnia, Old Baden, Chili, France—unpaid, French Colonies, Honduras, Mexico, Cuba, Porto Rico, Persia and a rare United States Justice Department, 12c. This packet is an excellent packet for a beginner. Price, post free, only $5.00.

Packet No. 34 contains 125 stamps from South and Central America. Price, post free, $2.00.

Packet No. 35 contains 50 stamps from the West Indian Islands, including rare surcharges of Port Rico, Old Cuba, Barbados, Bermuda, etc. Price only 85 cts.

Packet No. 36 contains 25 rare stamps from British North America, including New Brunswick, Nova Scotia, Newfoundland. Prince Edward Island, etc. Price, post free, $1.00.

Packet No. 37 contains 25 different United States Envelopes, including Centennial (2 var.) War and early issues. This packet is well recommended and worth the money. Price, 50c.

Packet No. 38 contains 75 varieties of Spain, including many rare ones and early issues. Price, post free, $1.00.

Packet No. 39 contains 20 United States Department stamps, including unused War, used Treasury, Agriculture, Navy, etc. Price, post free, 50c.

Packet No. 40 contains 40 varieties of Mexican stamps, including many scarce stamps. Price, post free, $1.00.

Packet No. 41 contains 20 stamps from Porto Rico. Price, post free, 35c.

Packet No. 42 contains 30 stamps from Cuba. Price, post free, 50c.

Packet No. 43 contains 50 unused stamps from Azores, Baden, Bavaria, Bolivia, Ecuador, Greece, Heligoland, Guatemala. Salvador, San Marino, etc. Price, post free, $1.00.

Packet No. 44 contains 30 varieties of United States Local stamps, including Allens, Boyds, Hussey, Swarts, Union Square, etc. Price, post free, 50c.

Packet No. 45 contains 20 varieties of U. S. Locals. Price, 25 cts.

Toronto Philatelic Journal.

OFFICIAL ORGAN OF CANADIAN PHILATELIC ASSOCIATION

VOL. 2   TORONTO, MAY, 1888.   No. 11.

San Salvador, 1879—Variations of Type.

BY HENRY HECHLER.

This issue of San Salvador shows variations in type as follows :—In the 1c. green there are two distinctly different type. They at first glance much resemble each other, but on close examination and comparison the differences are evident. The circles enclosing the figure of value in the upper left and lower right hand corners and the letter " c " in the other two corners, as well as the said figures and letters are larger in one than they are in the other. The lettering of the inscription on the oval band varies in the same way, while the sea in one is troubled by waves while in the other it is calm. There is also a difference in the shades of color, that of one being very light and the other a very dark green. Of the 2c. there are also two varieties with the same general differences as already observed in the 1c. with the addition that one kind has and the other has not a beaded line on either side connecting the ornamental scroll work below the squares in the upper corners with similar scroll work above the circles in the lower corners. There is a difference here in the shades of color, the one being rose and the other carmine. The same differences of type and color also occur in the 5c. blue, and in the higher values. Our philatelic friends will readily perceive these differences. These should be separately classed in catalogues as it is evident that different dies were used in producing them. The reasons for which is undoubtedly owing the first die being worn out or broken up when the first lot were printed necessitating the production of another when the first stock was used up.

The latest addition to the series is a 3c. brown bearing a figure of Liberty, and the 10c. orange, bearing a volcano and sea view, has changed to a new design. They are larger and of a neater design than than the old ones. Before long the new design will be extended to the other values which will then make a very pretty series, and will be welcomed by our philatelic friends.

When They Rush Things.

" Your duties must be somewhat monotonous," said a lady to a mailing clerk.

" They are indeed."

" The same round day after day, and week after week. No excitement."

" No excitement excepting when we have to rush things."

" And what is that !"

" Oh ! when we find ' In haste ' written on the outside of a letter."

" Oh ! yes that creates excitement."

" Tremendous."

THE C.P.A.

To the members of the C.P.A.

LADIES AND GENTLEMEN :—It is with feelings of pleasure that I look with extreme pride at the substantial growth our society has experienced, and I have still greater hopes that the coming fall will witness the joining of the 200th member. Each and every member can work to increase our membership in many ways. First, all who have correspondents should, when writing to such, add a word of commendation for the C. P. A., tell them of the advantages they will receive on payment of 25c per quarter. The success of our exchange department has been simply wonderful. Through it I have added many fine rare stamps to my collection and at the same time diminished my stock of duplicates without sacrificing them to a dealer.

I would suggest to our executive that they now abolish the 25c initation fee as the A. P. A. has done, and allow any member to pay quarterly or half-yearly. By so doing I think we will increase our membership, for any one joining will be so impressed with the advantages that for the sum of 25c. for three months they will not be without a C. P. A. membership certificate.

Complaints have come to me from several Ontario members about the following parties, and I would feel greatly obliged if any who know the parties or who can in any way give information to write me, and I will lay the whole matter before the Executive Board of the C.P.A., A. P. A.. and one of our large Continental societies :—Max Richter, Chemoritz, Saxony ; Jas. Steiner, Honolulu, Hawaii Islands ; J. B· Meyer, Constitucion 2, Callao, Peru ; Edward Heim, II Kleine Pfargarse. Vienna, Austria ; Benjamin & Bannister, 16 Bell Alley, London,Eng. ; Jacques Wortmann, Bucarest. Roumania.

I am glad to see that friend Hechler has endeavored to black list a number of these gentry, who seem to think that "distance lends enchantment," but having been elected honorary member for two or three foreign societies, I feel perfectly justified in the interest of the C. P. A. in carrying the war into their own country.

My hopes of harmony in the C. P. A. I am glad to say have been realized. While we are compartively strangers still I hope the bond of fraternal friendship shall never be broken, and with one and all members I wish them "good luck" and happy times while in the ranks of our socety. I have had the pleasure of visits from Librarian Walker, President Ketcheson. and others who have visited the capital, and found them gentlemen in the truest sense of the word, and any member visiting the capital will always find a warm friend in

Yours most truly,
JNO R. HOOPER,
Vice President C. P. A. Ont.
Ottawa, May 14th, 1888.

To the Members of the C.P.A.:

GENTLEMEN,—I am informed that a number of the members have not paid their annual dues yet, and I trust every member will send in his $1.00 to the Secretary at once. The fee is very small and will scarcely be adequate to meet the expenses of the Association, and so we cannot be expected to carry " dead-head " members, and all who do not pay at once will be suspended, and in one month more expelled.

The Exchange Superintendent informs me that we have been asked to join the International Exchange of the Dresden Society, and as the wider we can extend our exchange the better for our members, I am favorable to the scheme, and would like to have the opinion of the other officers.

We should arrange for time and place of our annual meeting soon, and I would like to receive suggestions from officers and members. I am pleased to inform you that our Association is growing steadily, and the future prospects are bright. The officers are all doing their utmost to further its interests, and if the members co-operate success is assured.

Yours truly,
H. F. KETCHESON,
Pres. C.P.A.

SECRETARY'S REPORT.

Our list of applications for membership this month gives the society good cause for congratulation. We have now 115 members and nine applicants No's 15, 50, 63 and 64 have resigned. The following have as yet failed to settle their accounts and in accordance with the notice given last month all who fail to pay up previous to June 10th will be suspended.

DELINQUENTS.

No's 7, 20, 21, 23, 24, 36, 40. 43, 54, 59, 68, 69, 71, 73, 74, 78, 81, 83, 84, 85, 86, 89, 94, 95, 96, 99, 103, 106, 110, 113, 114 and 116.

LIST OF NEW MEMBERS, NO. 3.

117—Jno. S. Bixby, 835 West Main St., Decatur, Ill.
118—Maurice E. Finney, Harrisburg, Pa.
119—C. C. Morency, Box 573, Quebec City.
120—W. D. Morton, care of Dr. Morton, Barrie, Ont.
121—F. Gottorf, cor. York and Caroline Sts., Hamilton.

LIST OF APPLICATIONS NO 3.

M. B. Holley, Traverse City, Mich. Reference, A. P. A.
W. C. Stone, Springfield, Mass. Reference, A. P. A.
Fred Harise, Charlottetown, P. E. I. Reference, W. Brown.
W. A. MacCalla, 237 Dock St., Phila., Pa. Reference, A. P. A.
A. A. Bartlett, Charlottetown, P.E.I. Reference W. Brown.
J. A. Shannon, Carbon, Wyo. References, E. W. Voute, T. P. Shannon.
F. N. Massoth, Jr., Hanover Centre, Ind. Reference, A.P.A.

E. J. Rogerson, Box 214, Barrie, Ont. References, G. A. Lowe, E. Y. Parker.
Felix Brande, Milford, Neb. Reference, P. M. Harper.

J. A. LEIGHTON,
Orangeville, May 11th, 1888.

LIBRARIAN'S REPORT.

I thought I would have been able to report this month a considerable increase in donations to the library, but the request I made last month was not responded to as liberally as I expected.

Photographs have been received during the month from W. D. B. Spry, N. E. Carter, and H. E. Deats.

Donations as follows : A. G. Nedham, 87 pieces ; N. E. Carter, 10; W. D. B. Spry and Henry S. Harte, 2 pieces.

Current Publications received : Toronto Philatelic Journal, The Philatelic World, The Canadian Philatelist, Collectors' Review, National Philatelist, Mohawk Standard, The Western Philatelist and Supplement to Philatelic Courier.

From the Publishers, catalogues of Eldredge & Williams, F. N. Massoth and R. R. Bogert & Co.'s Seventh Auction Sale.

GEORGE WALKER,
Librarian,
May 12th, 1888.

To the EDITOR TORONTO PHILATELIC JOURNAL.

SIR,—I hope all our C.P.A. members send in all their duplicate stamp magazines, catalogues, etc.. to Mr. Walker, Peterboro', Ont., our Librarian, and make this branch a success. Mr. Walker, will, I am sure, only be too happy to receive also photos of our members for the Library. The magnificent success of our Exchange Department, under Supt. Grenny, is astonishing, and all those members not participating are indeed missing a rare chance to get varieties for their collection. Yours philatelically,

J. R. HOOPER.

TORONTO
₽HILA₮ELIG ᴊOUℝNAL.

Published on the 1st of every month.

Geo. A. Lowe,   **Jos . Hooper,**
Eᴅ. PHILATELIᴄ DEᴾᴛ.   Eᴅ. NUMISMATIᴄ DEPT

SUBSCRITION :

United States and Canada 35c. per year ; Foreign Countries, 50c. per year.

Advertising Rates :

1 inch..	0 50
2 "	0 80
½ column	1 50
1 "	2 50
1 page..	4 50

10 per cent. discount on standing advts.
Copy wanted not later than the 25th.
Remit money by P.O. order, or small amounts in one or two cent stamps.
Address all correspondence to the

Toronto Philatelic Co.

106 Huron St.   **Toronto, Canada.**

TORONTO, MAY, 1888.

THE registration fee to the States has again been changed to 5c.

IF you wish to work up a good Canadian trade advertise in the Tᴏʀᴏɴᴛᴏ Pʜɪʟᴀ-ᴛᴇʟɪᴄ Jᴏᴜʀɴᴀʟ.

IT is understood the Postmaster-General is considering the advisability of making the three cent postal rate cover letters of an ounce in weight instead of half an ounce as at present.

Lᴀsᴛ week we had the pleasure of meeting Mr. M. D. Batchelder, President of the Batchelder Stamp Co., of St. Louis ; Mr. H. F. Ketcheson, of Belleville, President of the C.P.A.; Mr. E. J. Rogerson, of Barrie, member of C.P.A. All of whom were visiting this city.

A meeting of the stamp collectors of this city took place on the 18th inst. at the residence of Mr. E. Y. Parker. Mr· Ketcheson, President of the C.P.A., in the Chair. It was decided that the Toronto Philatelic Society should be reorganized.

Cᴏʟʟᴇᴄᴛᴏʀs should not be without Townsend's Philatelic Directory. It is the largest and most complete directory ever lished, containing the names and addresses of every Canadian Stamp Collector. If you have not already ordered one, send 25c. to George A. Lowe, 106 Huron St., Toronto, Canada, who is sole agent for the Dominion of Canada.

CORRESPONDENCE.

Letters of enquiry not aceompanied by 3c. for postage will be inserted under teis heading.

Wᴏᴏsᴛᴇʀ, Ohio, May 5th, 1888.
Gᴇɴᴛs,—In Tᴏʀᴏɴᴛᴏ Pʜɪʟᴀᴛᴇʟɪᴄ Jᴏᴜʀ-ɴᴀʟ you enquire for information about R. Vansyekel, Bridgetown, N. Y. I was cheated sometime ago by Vansyekel, Bridgeton, N.J., Brigen Co., and consider him a fraud. Hope this information may be of some use to you.
Respectfully,   W. S. Kɪɴᴢᴇʀ,

Hᴀʀᴛꜰᴏʀᴅ, Cᴏɴ.
Replying to " Canadensis," Edward Heim II. Vienna, Austria, is one of the largest and oldest stamp dealers in Europe. I recollect doing business with him fifteen years ago. He deals in rare stamps, current issues, *reprints and counterfeits.* He does an enormous business, and rarely answers letters inside of six weeks ; not then if a small order or you forget to enclose a stamp. He is, however, responsible. Young Canadian collectors want to go show in buying the " embossed " stamps of the United States. The market is full of counterfeits, and it is almost impossible to tell the difference. The ordinary embossing stamps used in some banks is identical in the comb impression

with that used on the stamps. I have one on my desk as I write, and I can remove a cancelled stamp from an envelope, emboss it, and gum it on again, and I myself could not pick it out if mixed with half a dozen genuine.

W. H. BRUCE.

Free Newspapers.

POSTMASTER PATTESON EXPRESSES HIMSELF WITH REGARD TO THE RUMOUR THAT A POSTAT RATE IS TO BE UPON ALL PERIODICALS.

Postmaster Patteson was endeavouring to calm the vehemence of a fussy old gentleman who was waging a controversy with him when a *Telegram* reporter entered his office this morning. The fussy old gentleman had a little dispute with the local post-office savings bank, and declared over and over that he would carry the matter before the House of Commons. The reporter looked out into the broad room towards the rear of the buildings, in which the distribution of the mail gathered in the city this morning was going on, and admired the suppleness of wrist and the precision of aim of the large staff of employes, who, stationed at tables in the centre of a wide circle, kept the air thick with letters flying to their proper receptacles. Hermann sends flights of cards all along the galleries of an opera house in showier, but really similar, way.

"Yes," said Mr. Patteson, when he was at leisure, "I have heard the rumour this morning that the Government are about to reduce general postage rates, and reimpose a moderate rate on newspapers sent direct from the office of publication, or in other words, abolish the free carrage of newspapers by the postal system of the country. I can't say what truth there is in the rumour. We haven't heard anything of it here yet. I can tell you the effect of the present law. It has been to inundate this office with tons—literally tons—of periodical printed matter, which cannot be regarded as newspapers or journals in any fair sense of the word. I may exercise a certain discretion, of course, but it only leads to unpleasantness." The postmaster showed the reporter several pamphlets and printed papers lying in his desk, which were advertisements.

"How is it that country postmasters' salaries depend largely upon the number of stamps they cancel?" he continued, repeating the reporter's question. "Well, the Department gets a return of the number of stamps cancelled in each office during an average month each year. They multiply this by 12, and size up the relative importance of the business through out the country by the figures thus obtained. Since the coming into force of the law allowing periodicals of all sorts, published at intervals of not less than once a month, to pass through the mails free, an enormous amount of work has been thrown upon country postmasters, for which they receive not a cent remuneration. It is argued not unreasonably that if the revenue is to be increased that they may be paid for the work they do, it should be increased at the expense of those benefitted. The system has been developing into a gigantic abuse, and I can't say myself that I should be sorry to see the old way returned to, although I consider that legitimate newspapers should be exempt." —*Telegram*.

C.P.A. Notes.

1. The 05 on 1 franc S.P.M. seems to be quite plentiful and there is a great discrepency in price in the exchange sheets on some at $1 each, and again on others at 40c. and 30c. each. The day has passed for getting $1 for this stamp.

2. A dearth of Canadian adhesive postage stamps of 1st. 2nd and 3rd issues, and an abundance of Canada Law and Bill Stamps is noticeable on the Exchange Sheets.

3. 1, 2 and 3rd. Musgrove's Business

College. The Badger State member is determined to make these "things" go. They now appear stuck on exchange sheets with perforations trimmed off—price 15c. each. The perf. variety at 10c. each did not appear to particularly strike the fancy of our collectors. How do they rank? Perhaps on a par with those beautiful Hamburg locals 116 for 1s. and 6d.

4. Some of the members do not seem to know the value of their stamps, and are fearful lest they should not mark them high enough. Keep the prices down if you wish to dispose of the stamps.

5. One or two more Ex-branches, say in Toronto and Montreal, is what we want, and would be much appreciated by your Ex-Supt.

6. Mr. Clotz, Supt. of Ex. A.P.A., is arranging for exchange with the I.P.V., Dresden, and would like the C.P.A. to become a complex or branch.

VEXATOR.

NUMISMATIC DEPARTMENT.

All matters relating to this department should be addressed to Jos Hooper, Box 145 Port Hope, Ont.

Whilst on a Numismatic tour recently we were very much surprised at the aimless, imperfect and unmethodical state of the large number of collections we reviewed, a lack of intelligent systemization was apparent everywhere. It is the intention of the Editor of this Department to give some helpful hints to collectors who are as yet in an embryo state, to try as far as his ability lies, to give foundation and progressive lessons that are essentially necessary to a true Numismatist. It is astonishing to see the number of small collectors scattered all over the land, a very imperfect idea of the vast extent and silent working of collectors is formed unless we start out "scatchel of duplicates in hand," and burrow from town to town, and house to house, with an energy without which we cannot succeed; very few houses in our land but has a few old coppers or silver pieces laid away as something curious, and very often an extensive notion of their value is estimated, it has been our happy lot to suggest and impart system and enthusiasm to a few inactives of this type who are now anxious and eager collectors, without true enthusiasm we cannot accomplish much, and then it must be of the lasting kind how many, as in religious matters, start fairly, but after the first brush of excitement over, give up or grow careless and indifferent. We are pleased that all are not thus; we have in our land Numismatics of long experience whose names might be mentioned, but will defer until we get permission permanent, lasting, durable. Enthusiasm must be based " Intelligent Knowledge," then " Sic Valeas " (Knowledge is Power") and becomes the true useful adjunct necessary to become a Coin Collector. Read up your guides before taking the journey; never take the journey without a knowledge of the road, although we believe the three-fourths of our collectors to-day started the wrong way, and in consequence have been mulcted to a large extent to our mind. Coin Collecting, without its foundation lessons, is like a young man starting to keep books without the thorough knowledge of the principles of book-keeping. With these remarks we enter on our labor of love entitled,

" HINTS TO COLLECTORS."
From Scott's Catalogue.

1. NUMISMATICS.—There are, upon a low estimate, ten thousand active collectors of Coins and Medals in the United States and Canada, whose cabinets represent, in intrinsic value, amounts from a few hundred dollars to many thousands. There are numerous collections which are valued above $5,000 while some reach as high as $25,000 and even $50,000.

Our principal cities have Societies devoted exclusively to the science of numismatics, embracing hundreds of members, while many others upon history, antiquity and kindred subjects, devote time and space to coins.

- 2. COLLECTING AS AN AMUSEMENT.— In foreign countries the forming of cabinets of coins has been a means of pleasant recreation and study for upwards of four hundred years. This pursuit has not been confined to any class, rank or position. The field for collectors is large and varied, extending from the period when the first metal took the shape and name of a coin seven hundred and fifty years before Christ, in an almost unbroken line, down to the present time. Without the existence of these numismatic treasures, history would have many blank pages to-day. It cannot be said that coins are without interest, or that they possess less fascination, than other objects of curious research whether antique, mediæval or modern. They lead to such a knowledge of history and art, as cannot otherwise be obtained. There is no truer saying than that "we all have our hobbies." Hence we speak a word for Numismatics, commending the same to your careful consideration, asserting that it will be found entertaining and instructive to a degree that challenges all other science or pursuits.

3. WHAT GIVES A COIN VALUE.—The age of a coin is not conclusive to establish rarity ; it is the historic interest it may possess, or the limited number struck, which will make it sought after by a large number of collectors. A coin of Augustus, the first Roman Emperor, B. C. 27 to A. D. 14, is obtainable in fair condition for 50 cents, while the 20 cent pieces from the U. S. Mint of 1877 and 1878 command from ten to fifteen times their face value. To go back a little further, a United States cent of almost any date between 1793 and 1814 in perfect state of preservation, is worth $5.00, while some of the dates within this period are worth very much more— $25.00 is not an uncommon price for the cents of 1793, 1799 and 1804.

Condition, or more plainly, the state of preservation, always *regulates the price* of a coin ; it has the greatest bearing however on the rare issues which multiply rapidly in value as they approach perfection ; this means *mint* state and positively unworn. If scratched corroded, spotted, or stained, however slightly, its value is impaired.

Philatelic Tid-Bits.

HENRY S. HARTE.

The inventor of the stamped newspaper wrapper is said to have been one Augustine Watson, of Washington, D.C.

Cyrus, King of Persia, is the traditional author of the first postal service.

The first Postmaster-General of England was Thomas Randolph ; appointed by Queen Elizabeth in 1581.

The first adhesive envelope is said to have been used in England in 1848.

The penny stamps of Great Britain appeared with letters in each corner in June, 1864.

The "Mauritius" collection of stamps contained a sheet each of "F F" 5c. "L.S." 10c. and "L S."5c. Canadian Law Stamps rouletted instead of perforated.

SILK RIBBONS !

Batchelder Postage Stamp Company,

2006 GRAND AV., ST. LOUIS, MO., U.S.

WHOLESALE PRICE LIST

These prices are made to dealers only. Orders under $1.00 respectfully declined.
Wholesale list sent free on application.

UNUSED STAMPS.

	Per 10	Per 100
Allen's Locals, red or yellow...	10	75

USED STAMPS.

Our selections of used stamps are guaranteed to be far superior to any other wholesale dealers. We will at all times guarantee our patrons fine mixtures. If in some instances our prices are a little higher, the mixture is enough better to pay for the addition in prices.

	Per 10	Per 100
Argentine Republic, well assorted	$0 10	$0 75
Austria, well assorted		15
Austrian Italy, well assorted	07	50
Azores, well assorted	15	
Baden, " "	10	70
Barbados " "	06	35
Bermuda " "	12	1 00
Brazil " "	07	40
Bolivia " "	35	
Bosnia " "	15	1 00
Br. Guiana " "		25
Bulgaria " "	10	80
Cape of Good Hope, well assorted		30
Central America, finely assorted		1 50
Ceylon, 72, 2c.	10	
" 5c.		60
" 2, 4 and 8c.		25
" 5c. on 8c.	10	75
" 5c. on 64c.	1 00	
Chili, 5c. assorted		25
Costa Rica, 1c., green	10	
" " 2c., red	15	
Cuba, 1857	10	
" 1864, green ane pink assorted	20	
" 1869, 10c. brown	12	
" 1870, 10c. green	12	
" 1871, 25c. blue	12	
" 1873, 25c., lilac	15	
" well mixed, 57-82		60
Cyprus, ½p, green	10	70
Denmark, assorted		10
Dominican Republic, 1c., 1885	20	
Eastern Roumelia, well assorted	15	
Ecuador, 5c., blue	10	80
Egypt, well assorted		50
Finland, " "		25
France, 77, 30-40-75c., 1f.		40
Greece, well assorted		25
Hong Kong, well assorted	12	1 00
Honduras, " "	15	1 30
Iceland, 10a	20	
India, well assorted		25
Italy, segnatasse well assorted	05	30
India, H. M. S., assorted		20
Jamaica, well assorted		30
Japan, " "	06	40
" 2c, red		25
Muritius, 79, 4c.	10	
" 80, 2c.	15	
Mexico, 1851, 5c., brown	20	1 75
" 1874, 25c	07	60
" 1875, 50c., green	50	
" 2878, 10, orange	10	1 00
" 1880, 4c	80	7 00
" 1879, 5c. orange	10	
" 1879, 10c. blue	15	
" 1884, 1c. green	08	75
" 2c., green	10	1 00
" 3., green	20	1 70
" 4c "	15	
" 1c "	30	
" 10c "	05	
" " 20c "	30	
" " 25c green	50	
" " well assorted		90
" 1885, 2c., rose	15	
" " 3c., brown	25	2 00
" " 4c., salmon	60	5 00
" " 5c., blue	15	
" " 6c., brown	25	2 00
" " 10c., orange	15	
" " well assorted		1 20
" 1886. 1c., green	08	60
" " 2c., rose	10	90
" " 3c., lilac	12	1 00
" " 4c., lilac	20	
" " 5c., blue	08	75
" " 6c	15	
" " 10c. lilac	07	05
" Official, 1886, red	35	2 00
" well assorted, no 1p	20	
Natal, 1874, 1p, carmine	05	40
Norway, finely assorted		20
New South Wales, 1p and 2p		20
New Zealand, 1p and 2p		20
Persia, well assorted	20	1 75
Portugal " "		20
Porto Rico, 4 var. 25 surcharg'd	20	1 50
Porto Rico, 1876, surcharged cross paraph.	30	
" " 25, blue 1877	06	50
" " 1878, 25c., green	06	40
" " 1879, 25c.	07	
" " 1882, 1c. green	07	
" " 2m., purple	07	
Porto Rico, " 5c., blue	04	25
" " well assorted		40
Queensland, assorted		20
Roumania, well assorted		20
Russia		15
South Australia, 1p and 2p		20
Servia, well assorted		50
Spain, " "		15
Spain, war, well assorted		15
Straits Settlements, well ass't'd	12	10
Switzerland, well assorted		25
Tasmania, " "		10
Trinidad, assorted		50
Turkey, well as'td, old and new	10	
United States of Columbia, astd	10	
Venezuela, assorted	10	
Victoria, "	08	30
Western Australia, 1p and 2p	07	45
United States, Postoffice, 3c.	05	35
" " Interior, 3c.	06	40
" " Treasury, 3 and 6c	10	90
" " 6 var		2 00
" " War, 1c	15	1 00
" " 2c	15	1 00
" " 3 and 6c		70
" " envelopes		60
" " Locals, well as'td		1 25
" " Centennial, 3c. green and red		1 25
" Agriculture	30	

(Continued from preceding page.)

Well Mixed--Suitable for Sheets.

	Per 10	Per 100		Per 10	Per 100
To sell at 1c. each		30	To sell at 4 and 5c. each	20	1 50
" " " 2c. "	10	60	" " " 8 to 10c. "	40	3 50
" " " 3c. "	12	1 00			

Well Assorted Continentals.

10,000......................$1 75 ; 25,000......................$3 00 ; 100,000 ....$10 00

Blank Approval Sheets.

Ruled in two colors to hold 40 stamps. Sample free. Prices: 25 for 15c ; 50, 25c ; 100 50c ; 500, $2. Sent post free on receipt of price.

YOUNG AMERICAN POSTAGE STAMP ALBUM.

Contains space for 2000 stamps.

This book fills a want long felt by beginners, who wish a cheap book. or for those who wish a cheap book to put in their duplicates. Stamp-issuing countries in alphabetical order. Plenty of room for all new issues. The best, cheapest and handsomest book ever made for the price. Price 25 cents. By mail 28 cents. This book contains some novel features never before introduced.

HALF DIME SETS.

The left-hand figure denotes the number of varieties in each set. Price 5c. a set. Five sets 25c., 12 sets 50c. or the entire lot, 61 sets, containing 310 stamps, sent post free for $2.65.

To every person purchasing the entire lot we will give a Triangle Newfoundland stamp. This stamp retails for 25c.

5 Argentine.	2 Monaco.	4 Egypt.	4 Tasmania.	4 Peru.
4 Austria and Italy.	5 Porto Rico.	5 Finland.	3 Trinidad.	8 Russia.
10 Austria.	7 Portugal.	10 France.	2 Grenada.	3 Venezuela.
8 Australia.	4 Prussia.	3 French Colonies.	5 Greece.	8 Victoria.
3 Bermuda.	9 Russia.	10 Denmark.	10 Holland.	8 Wurtemberg.
4 Barbados.	5 Sardinia.	5 Sardinia.	10 Great Britain	10 U.S. Postage.
4 Baden.	3 Straits Settlements.	3 Sandwich Isles.	3 Hong Kong.	10 U.S. Envelope.
3 Bulgaria.	4 Ceylon.	5 Servia.	2 Iceland.	5 U.S. Departments.
5 Brazil.	2 Confederate.	10 Spain.	5 India.	4 U.S. War.
5 Bosnia.	2 Cyprus.	8 Sweden.	2 Italy.	3 Hamburg.
5 Chili.	5 Cape of Good Hope.	4 Sweden Official.	4 Jamaica.	
7 Canada.	4 Cuba	10 Swiss.	4 Japan.	
6 Mexico.	3 Dutch Indies.	5 Turkey.	5 Luxemburg.	

DIME SETS.

The left hand figure denotes the number of varieties in each set. Price 10 cents a set, 5 sets for 50 cents, 11 sets for $1.00 or the entire lot of 73 sets containing 457 stamps sent post free for $6.35.

To any person purchasing the entire lot we will give an Argentine Republic 60 cents stamp. This stamp retails for 50c.

15 Australian.	5 Bulgaria.	4 France unpaid.	10 Porto Rico.	8 Victoria.
3 Alsace and Loraine.	7 Brazil.	6 French Colonies.	5 Orange States.	8 U.S. Officials.
3 Angola.	4 Br. Guiana.	7 Finland.	3 Paraguay.	15 U.S Revenues.
7 Argentine Republic.	10 Canada	15 Great Britain.	2 Fiji Isles.	5 U.S. of Columbia.
20 Austria.	8 Canada Bill.	4 Guatemala.	2 Peru.	3 Trinidad.
6 Austria and Italy.	3 Canada Law.	7 Greece.	5 Servia.	6 Sweden Losen.
4 Azores.	7 Cape of Good Hope.	3 Hayti.	17 Spain.	6 Sweden Official
6 Baden.	6 Ceylon.	5 Hong Kong.	5 Sandwich Isles.	2 Philippine Isles.
7 Barbados.	6 Chili.	4 Heligoland.	5 Saxony.	3 Nicaragua.
5 Bergedorf.	2 Persia.	7 Japan.	8 Roman States.	4 Natal.
7 Bavaria.	2 Congo.	8 Jamaica.	7 Roumania.	5 Ecuador.
6 Bavaria Return Letter	7 Cuba.	10 India.	6 Turkey.	
3 Bahamas.	4 Eastern Roumelia.	10 Mexico.	2 Simoor.	
4 Bermuda.	7 Egypt.	4 Monaco.	5 Straits Settlements.	
5 Bosnia.	20 France.	4 Newfoundland.	5 Venezuela.	

Special attention is called to the above 5 and 10 cent sets. The stamps are all guaranteed genuine and if desired a written guarantee will be sent with each order. Your attention is called to the number of varieties in each set and and if the same stamps were to be sold single they would bring twice as much as we get for them when put up in sets.

BARGAINS

GOOD TILL JULY 15TH

4 var. Persia Official, 1881	$0 15	7 " Bulgaria	10
15 " Mexico	15	1 " 1c. U. S. Periodical	15
15 " Porto Rico	20	6 " Mexico Porte D. Mar, colored	35
2 " Mexico ruled paper	25		
25 " Mexico	50	United States Interior—complete set	1 50
40 " Mexico	1 00	" " State " "	5 00
3 " Salvador, 1867	10	" " Post Office " "	2 00
5 " Guatemala, 1882, unused	10	" " War " "	75
4 " Nicaragua unused	40	All above unused.	

JUNE   1888.

Toronto

Philatelic Journal

A Monthly Magazine For Stamp Collectors

NORTH AMERICA

SOUTH AMERICA

TORONTO PHILATELIC CO
106 HURON STREET.

TORONTO CANADA.

TOR. ENG. CO.

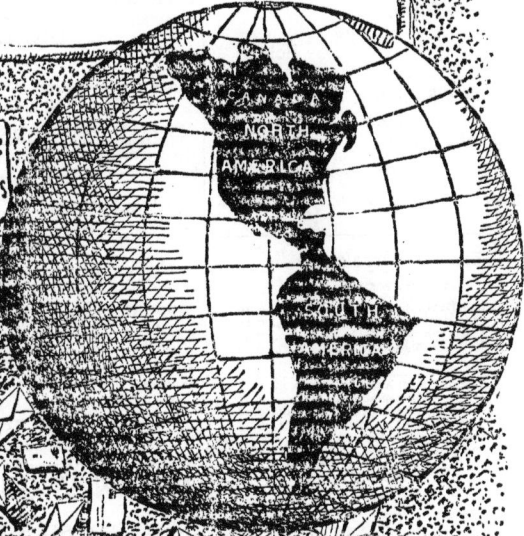

IMPORTANT NOTICE.

I MUST hereby thank my many friends and patrons for the kind support tendered me in my business during the past few years, which I must say has been beyond my most sanguine expectations.

I regret to announce that Mr. Dill, who has been with me for the past eight months, has been unable to continue in the business on account of sickness in his family, which caused him to give up all business duties.

In the future Mr. Wm. C. Atcheson will manage the stamp business with the aid of Geo. W. Atcheson. Mr. Atcheson is a prominent philatelist and I feel sure that my many patrons will continue their favors, assuring them that all orders will be filled promptly. I remain yours philatelically,

M. D. BATCHELDER.

BATCHELDER'S
MOUND CITY POPULAR PACKETS.

Packet No. 32 contains 1,000 different postage stamps, being a complete collection in itself. This packet contains many rare stamps, among which are, Argentine, 90c. Cape of Good Hope, Triangular, Newfoundland, (Triangular), China, Cuba, Ceylon, rare surcharges.

Ecuador, Mexican—many varieties. Persia Official, United States Newspaper stamps, also obsolete envelopes. State Department, unused and other excellent stamps. We will send this packet post free, and registered for $10.

Packet No. 33 contains 500 different stamps, including Argentine, Azores, Brazil, Bulgaria, Bosnia, Old Baden, Chili, France—unpaid, French Colonies, Honduras, Mexico, Cuba, Porto Rico, Persia and a rare United States Justice Department, 12c. This packet is an excellent packet for a beginner. Price, post free, only $5.00.

Packet No. 34 contains 125 stamps from South and Central America. Price, post free, $2.00.

Packet No. 35 contains 50 stamps from the West Indian Islands, including rare surcharges of Port Rico, Old Cuba, Barbados, Bermuda, etc. Price only 85 cts.

Packet No. 36 contains 25 rare stamps from British North America, including New Brunswick, Nova Scotia, Newfoundland, Prince Edward Island, etc. Price, post free, $1.00.

Packet No. 37 contains 25 different United States Envelopes, including Centennial (2 var.) War and early issues. This packet is well recommended and worth the money. Price, 50c.

Packet No. 38 contains 75 varieties of Spain, including many rare ones and early issues. Price, post free, $1.00.

Packet No. 39 contains 20 United States Department stamps, including unused War, used Treasury, Agriculture, Navy, etc. Price, post free, 50c.

Packet No. 40 contains 40 varieties of Mexican stamps, including many scarce stamps. Price, post free, $1.00.

Packet No. 41 contains 20 stamps from Porto Rico. Price, post free, 35c.

Packet No. 42 contains 30 stamps from Cuba. Price, post free, 50c.

Packet No. 43 contains 50 unused stamps from Azores, Baden, Bavaria, Bolivia, Ecuador, Greece, Heligoland, Guatemala, Salvador, San Marino, etc. Price, post free, $1.00.

Packet No. 44 contains 30 varieties of United States Local stamps, including Allens, Boyds, Hussey, Swarts, Union Square, etc. Price, post free, 50c.

Packet No. 45 contains 20 varieties of U. S. Locals. Price, 25 cts.

Toronto Philatelic Journal.

OFFICIAL ORGAN OF CANADIAN PHILATELIC ASSOCIATION

Vol. 2   TORONTO JUNE, 1888.   No. 12

Letter from the Vice-President of Nova Scotia.

——

DEAR EDITOR,—As you do not appear to be troubled with many letters from Nova Scotia, I made up my mind to write you one on matters in general.

Our Canadian Association is now an accomplished fact, and I think we may justly congratulate ourselves upon the success of the movement which has thus banded the stamp collectors of Canada into one general association.

I am finding evidence almost every week of the interest that is being awakened in the minds of old time collectors who have long been slumbering, but are again coming to the front and taking up their old hobby with renewed vigor.

This new inspiration is mainly due to the increased importance which our common bond of brotherhood gives us.

I have talked to several old collectors within a few weeks, who for years have not added a stamp to their collections. In fact had almost forgotten the existence of that evidence of youthful folly. But are now coming rapidly into line, and intend to identify themselves with us and try to regain their lost ground.

The lasting benefits that this increased interest will confer on the Association are apparent.

While some of those ancient collectors will doubtless tire of the work and crease to be very active our membership will at least gain temporarily.

But the more important point is that many old collections thus resurrected will find their way into the hands of live collectors which would otherwise long "lie deeply hidden from human eye." Thus we will all be benefited more or less directly.

Now for another point I wish to touch upon : Our very efficient and painstaking Exchange Supetintendent evidently has his department in full swing. I have seen several of the books and covers on circuit and while some of them are very creditable I am compelled to say that they contain too large a proportion of the veriest trash imaginable.

This association is not composed of boys. Stamp collecting is no longer child's play. In these latter days stamp collectors to be successful require brains, industry, education or intelligence and some money.

Our associotion is largely composed of men who make Philately a study for the pleasure and profit they draw from it. Men who are will to spend some time and some money in their pleasant pursuit. Then why afflict them by sending out such sheets as those of forty (40) stamps —total value $1.25 to $1.50 and so on up to $2.00.

What can a collector, having over 3,000 in his album, want of such sheets they get

to be regular old '' chestnuts '' long before
that number is reached.

I hope that in course of time the
quality of our sheets will improve for it
certainly should not take long to convince
those who make up cheap and trashy
sheets that our members do not want
them.

Another difficulty is pricing rare stamps.
Members putting rare stamps on their
sheets naturally want to secure the highest
price possible, and thus when catalogue
prices are once departed from there is no
limit to the extravagent values that are
placed on sheets of more or less rarity.

At this moment I am not prepared to
suggest any plan for regulating this ques·
tion of values.

I think this matter is one of the most
important that the association will have
deal with at its annual communication.

And now for a look at the Nova Scotia
Branch Society for a moment : I had the
pleasure of presiding at its last regular
meeting in May and I assure you it afforded me great satisfaction. I find the members fully alive to their work. The average intelligence and standing of the members is high, and they follow their private
study most perseveringly. I venture to
say that there is in the N.S.P.A. the
material for some eminent Philatelists.

I trust when the place and time of our
annual meeting is decided upon that it will
be a brilliant success, for there is nothing
like personal intercourse of its members to
benefit the association. The meeting together and interchange of thoughts and
opinions are of more practical value than
all the correspondence of a decade. I
shall attend if possible wherever the meeting is called.

Trusting, Mr. Editor, that I have not
taken too much of your space.

I remain yours, respectfully,

A. J. CRAIG.

THE C.P.A.

SECRETARY'S REPORT.

Although our membership is not as
large as it was last month, we have the
satisfaction of knowing that all we have
are live active philatelists, possessing
enough interest in the Society to pay the
small annual dues. Our membership is
now 112, and the number of applications
is identical with that of last month. I
now give notice that the following have
been expelled from the Society for non-
payment of dues : Nos. 36, 40, 59, 69,
74, 78, 81, 84, 85, 96. No. 73 has
resigned. We have decided to admit
members for balance of year at 50c. and
trust many will take this opportunity of
joining.

LIST OF NEW MEMBERS, NO. 4.

122—M. B. Holley, Traverse City, Mich.
123—W. C. Stone, Springfield, Mass.
124 - Fred. Harvie, Charlottetown, P.E.I.
125—W. A. McCalla, 237 Dock St.,
     Philadelphia, Pa.
126—A. A.Bartlett, Charlottetown, P.E.I.
127—J. A. Shannon, Carbon, Wyo.
128—F. N. Mossoth, Jr., Hanover Centre,
     Ind.
129—E. J. Rogerson,Box 214, Barrie,Ont.
130— Felix Brande, Milford, Neb.

LIST OF APPLICATIONS, NO. 4.

A. E. Labelle, care A. W. Ogilvie &
Co., Montreal. Reference—H. F. Ketcheson, J. A. Leighton.

S. G. Retallock, Box 576, Belleville,
Ont. Referinces—H. F. Ketcheson, J.
A. Leighton.

Jesse E. Harpel. 22 S. Centre St., Potts-
ville, Pa. Reference—F. S. Goldbury,
T. M. Snyder.

W. S. Aldrich, Box 576, Portland,
Maine. Reference—A.P.A.

F. W. Feldwisch, Box 2922, Denver,
Col. Reference—A.P.A.

H. Morell, 76 Baldwin St., Toronto, Ont. Reference—E. Y. Parker.

Geo. N. Campbell, M.D., Lock Box 87, Hopkinsville, Ky. Reference—A.P.A.

J. E. Schultze, Box 1570, Montreal, P. Q. Reference A. E. Warren, R.A.B. Hart.

Geo. D. Ives, Pictou, N.S.

Mr. Cleo. C. Morency's address, published last month as Box 573 Quebec, should have been Box 513.

The address of Mr. J. H. Todd has been changed from Hector to Banff.

J. A. LEIGHTON.
Orangeville, June 12th, 1888.

LIBRARIAN'S REPORT.

GENTLEMEN, — I am very much pleased to report that President Ketcheson has offered to donate a blank album to the library for the purpose of forming a collection of Canadian stamps. I will be pleased to have the members send any duplicates of Canada stamps they may have to spare. Who will make first donation to the society's album.

If the officers of the C.P.A. who have not already done so will send their photographs I will have them grouped and framed, and will forward it to our first Annual Convention for exhibition. Come, Mr. Officials, as well as members, send along your photographs. The last month has been very cold as far as photographs of members was concerned, the library did not see a new face.

Donations received as follows : F. J. Grenny, 25 pieces ; N. E. Carter, 8 pieces ; J. C. Niesser, 12 pieces ; Mr. Patrick Chalmers, 1 ; R. R. Bogert & Co Catalogue of eight auction sale.

Current journals received were Toronto Philatelic Journal, Canada Stamp and Coin Journal, Plain Talk, the Philatelic World, Hawkeye State Collector, the National Philatelist and last but not least, The Stamp.

GEO. WALKER,
Librarian.

Philatelic Notes.

Mr. John R. Hooper, Vice-President C.P.A., has been elected an honorary member of the great Amsterdam Society of Philatelists, which is named the "Nederlansche Vereeniging van Postzegel-versamelaars." This society is one of the most select and best organized in the world. Among its members are J. B. Moens, of Brussels ; A. Huart, of Amsterdam ; the Duke of Liria, Madrid ; the Baroness v. de Wolkoff, Paris ; Col. Romswinkel, Padang and other dignitaries. Mr. Hooper is the first and only Canadian so honored by this society. Messrs. Rechert and Lohmeyer are the sole attached members in the U.S.

There is agitation now going on as to when and where our C.P.A. Convention will be held. Some say Montreal, others Toronto. The former place would be more central if the Maritime men would attend. An expression of opinion from our officers would be in order.

The three latest surcharges from Colombo, Ceylon, are the 4c. rose and 4c. mauve. They also appear in inverted type, all surcharged "Two Cents," in black over old value.

Among the most recent discoveries and extreme rarities in the possession of a C.P.A. member is an unsevered pair of unused, ungummed and unperforated $3 third issue Can. bill stamps ; a $5 unused Supreme Court stamp and an unused $3 bill surcharged "N.S." The first is an error off one sheet destroyed by the officials, the remander being regular issues rarely met with.

TORONTO
ℙHILATELIC JOURNAL.

Published on the 1st of every month.

Geo. A. Lowe,   **Jos . Hooper,**
ED. PHILATELIC DEPT.   ED. NUMISMATIC DEPT

SUBSCRIPTION :
United States and Canada 35c. per year ; Foreign Countries,
50c. per year.

Advertising Rates :

1 inch	0 50
2 "	0 80
½ column	1 50
1 "	2 50
1 page	4 50

10 per cent. discount on standing advts.
Copy wanted not later than the 25th.
Remit money by P.O. order, or small amounts in one or
two cent stamps.
Address all correspondence to the

Toronto Philatelic Co.
106 Huron St.   Toronto. Canada.

TORONTO, JUNE, 1888.

OUR next number will contain an interesting philatelic story by Mrs. Julia S. Mason, entitled " From Under the Hammer."

SUBSCRIBERS or members not receiving their copies regular will please notify us of the fact, and we will have same rectified

WE had the pleasure of meeting Mr. W. D. Boyd, member of C. P. A., of Simcoe, last week. Give us a call, Philatelists, when in this city. We are always pleased to meet you.

WITH this number we complete our second volume. We beg to thank our patrons for the hearty support tendered us during the past few years. We also thank the members of the C.P.A. for the distinction conferred upon us at the last election, in selecting us to serve as Official Organ for so important an Association. We trust that you will continue to favor us with your support and we can assure you it will always be our aim to make the TORONTO PHILATELIC JOURNAL the leading philatelic paper of this country.

THE leading topic among stamp collectors is, where and when is the first Convention of the C.P.A to be held? It will likely be decided either in favor of Montreal or Toronto, the latter seems most probable. There are many reasons why Toronto shoul be chosen in preference to the former—in the first place, it is the most central city in Canada, and more accessible to our American members than any other. Again our sights are more numerous, and the hotel accommodation is far superior and more reasonable than elsewhere. If held in Toronto during September cheap cheap travelling rates could se secured, and would thus give members an opportunity of attending our great Industrial Exhibition to be held here in that month.

A MEETING of the stamp collectors of this city was held on the evening of the 7th inst , at the residence of Mrs. Mason, for the object of reorganizing the Toronto Philatelic Society. The meeting was called to order at 8 p.m. with Mr. Mc. Minn in the chair. The following officers were elected for the ensuing year: President, T. J. McMinn ; Vice-President,

Geo. A. Lowe ; Secretary-Treasurer, H. Morrell ; Executive Committee, Mrs. Mason, E. Y. Parker, W. Wilby. Meetings to be held first Monday in each month. On account of first Monday in July being a public holiday the next meeting will be postponed till the following Monday (9 inst.) at the residence of Mrs. Mason, 362 Yonge Street.

CORRESPONDENCE.

Letters of enquiry not accompanied by 3c. for postage will be answered under this heading.

DEAR SIR,—I notice that the Exchange Superintendent has been requested to join the International Exchange of the Dresden Society. I think it a very good plan, for the members could then have a much wider and larger field to circulate their duplicates in and thus make more out of their exchanges, as the members of the C.P.A. are comparatively few yet, and a great quantity of stamps can not be circulated to any good effect.

The C.P.A. Exchange Dept. is however a grand success so far, and I look anxiously for more book to come along. There are not so many rare stamps on the sheets as are desirable, but many good and rare speciments can be obtained, so all interested should not fail to participate in the exchange.

Yours truly,
N. E. CARTER,
Delavan, Wis., June 2, 1888.

P.S.—I have the 10c. current U.S. stamp, double perforated. I have never seen it mentioned in any journal, so I consider it quite rare. N. E. CARTER.

N.B. Vice-President's Letter.

To the Members of the C.P.A.:

GENTLEMEN,—Is it not time that the question when and where the first annual Convention of the C.P.A. should be held should come up for discussion ? The general understanding, I think, last winter was that It would be held in Montreal or Toronto in January, 1889. Now is not January, or in fact any of the winter months, a wrong time in which to hold this convention ? It is well known that during the winter months, many at a distance would not be able at attend, and besides this, the modes of transit are not at all times to be relied upon ; for instance, it might happen that a big snowstorm might come and block up the northern branch of the I. C. R., as it has frequently done in the past for a week or so, consequently the members of our Association from the Maritime Provinces would be unable to attend. Would it not therefore be much better to postpone the Convention until June, 1889, or to hold it this fall, say in Sept. or Oct.

Further, as regards the place where it will be held, is not Montreal preferable to Toronto ? The former, I think, is more of a centre than the latter place, and to a great extent more easy of access to the majority of our members.

I should like to hear what there is to be said upon this matter, and would for my part be much in favor of holding the Convention in Montreal about the 15th of next September.

Believe me, Gentlemen,
Yours, fraternally,
HENRY S. HARTE,
Prov. Vice-Pr. for N.B.
Petitcodiac, N.B., June 1st, 1888.

A Letter from John R. Hooper.

To the Members of the C.P.A.:

LADIES AND GENTLEMEN,—Last month I requested all philatelists, whether belonging to the society or not, to send me information concerning the following parties:—Max Richter, Chemnitz, Saxony ; Jas. Steiner, Honolulu, Hawaii Islands ; J. B. Meyer, Callao, Peru ; Ed. Heim, Vienna, Austria ; Benjamin & Bannister, Moorgate St., London, Eng.; Jacques Wortmann, Bucarest, Roumania; J. Escalante, Venoro XIV., Mexico; Miss Jessie E. Greene, Denton, Nebraska ; Geo. Z. Anderson, Louisville, Ky.

To the list published I have added three names. Now, as *all* the above parties have had dealings with the C.P.A. members, I hope any one who is acquainted will write me all the information they can.

From Mr. W. H. Bruce, I see that one of the number referred to above (Ed. Heim, II. Kleine Pfargasse, Vienna, Austria) deals in *counterfeits.* I am glad to receive this valuable information.

I particularly warn collectors to beware of the party calling themselves *Miss (?) Jessie E. Green,* and hailing from Denton, Lancaster Co., Neb. This party I intend to prosecute, and have already made complaints to the head postal authorities at Washington, and also to the U.S. marshal in Lancaster county. The *Hawkeye State Collector* throws some light on the mystic Miss Greene, and in conjunction with the authorities I hope to place this swindler in the arms of the law. The reference this party has been giving is J. J. Winters, attorney-at-law, of Denton. Further interesting developments anxiously expected.

Yours Philatelically,
John R. HOOPER,

Vice-Pr. Ont. C.P.A., Ottawa, Ont.

Canadian Postage Stamps.

BY CANADENSIS.

By the Dominion Auditor-General's Report considerable information of interest to philatelists is contained therein. The largest number of any particular denomination of stamps issued was the 3c., while the 15c. is the least in demand. For every 5c. registered letter stamp used there are eight 2c. registered stamps. The ordinary stamps from ½c. to 15c. cost 25c. per 1000, and 50c. per 1,000 for registered stamps ; 1c. postcards cost the Government $1.25 per 1,000 ; the 2c. $3.50 per 1,000 ; reply cards, $3.25 per 1,000 ; wrappers, $2 per 1,000 : 1c. and 3c. envelopes (No. 1 size) $3 per 1,000 ; 3c. envelopes (No. 2 size) $3.50 per 1,000. For each new plate it costs $150; the registered letter plates being valued at $75 each. The following table will show the comparative number of stamps issued and hence their scarcity :

½ cent postage stamps		......	650,000
1	do	......	39,475,000
2	do	......	3,350,000
3	do	......	62,300,000
5	do	......	2,750,000
6	do	......	1,150,000
10	do	......	300,000
15	do	......	135,000

Total.....................110,110,000

2 cent registered letter stamps			3,20,000
5	do	do	400,000

Total........................ 3,600,000

1 cent post cards		....	16,971,000
2	do	....	70,000
Reply cards		....	175,000
Post bands		....	595,000
1 cent envelopes, No. 1		.....	197,000
3	do	No. 1	190,000
3	do	No. 2	80,000

Women in the English Post Office.

Mrs. Millicent Fawcett, widow of the blind Postmaster-General of England, talks of coming to this country to give a course of lectures. She is and has been for years profoundly interested in everything concerning the advancement of her sex, and it was owing to her influence that her husband, upon assuming the Postmaster-Generalship, threw open the appointnents to unrestricted competition and strove long and earnestly to have the wages of women employed in the postoffice greatly increased. Mr. Fawcett was totally blind when he assumed the responsible position of controlling the British postal system, but his energetic and devoted wife supplied him with eyes and was so helpful and skilful that he carried on the department to the entire satisfaction of the public and the authorities. Until Mr. Fawcett's appointment it was difficult for women to get positions in the post-offices, and three nominees competent for each appointment. He abolished the system of nomination altogether, and competitors were subject to only three conditions—that their ages must be no less than 18 or more than 20, and only widows and single women were eligible, and that they must be duly qualified in respect to health and character. Arithmetic, English composition, geography, history and chirography are the subjects of their competitive examinations. When Mr. Fawcett entered upon his duties the initial salary of the second-class female clerk was £40. By his urgent appeal this was raised to £65 for London clerkships, with a yearly increase of £3 until they reach £80. In Edinburgh and Dublin the salary begins at £55 and rises to £60. Promotion to a higher class of service obtains higher salaries. The highest salary earned by any woman is in the general postoffice, and amounts to £300. In the Government reports the work of the women clerks is referred to as particularly good and quite equal to that of the men, their salaries, however, remaining but one-third of what is paid to the men. This injustice Mrs. Fawcett has devoted years of effort to abolish, and though only in very few instances has there been any movement towards equalisation, she is not discouraged but firmly believes that evantually clerks will be estimated and rewarded solely by the work they do and not by a mere question of sex. All told, there are 2,981 women employed by the postoffice of the United Kingdom, 750 being in the central establishments of London, Edinburgh and Dublin, and thirty-six in the Provinces. The rest are in the savings bank and telegraphic departments.

Languages of the World.

Chinese is the most popular language in the world. It is spoken by 400,000,-000 persons. Hindostani by upwards of 100,000,000; English by more than 100,-000,000 ; English by more than 100,000,-000 ; Russian by more than 70,000,000 ; German by 58,000,000 ; Spanish by 48,-000,000 ; and French by only 40,000,000. —*Ex.*

—Rudolf Schoot is a Cleveland laborer. While preparing the foundation for a house, dug up a rusty tin box in which were 700 silver dollars of the mintage of 1864. He handed them over to the owner of the property. His honesty was rewarded with the gift of a dollar.

--Invitations to a ball given by a colored society of Fort Dodge, Iowa, contained the information that no distinction would be make between plain and colored people.

···Eighteen young men of Mountain Home, Ark., swore off from the tobacco habit on the first of the present year. Whoever returns to the habit is to be ducked in a pond of water.

— A girl in Oconee county, Ga., married at the age of nine years, her husband being 45 years years old.

Work up a good Canadian trade by advertising in the TORONTO PHILATELIC JOURNAL. Mrs. J. S. Mason, stamp dealer, says, " I am very well satisfied with my advertisement, having received dozens of orders from it. I enclose you an advt. to stand six months."

SILK RIBBONS !

Those of our lady readers who would like to have an elegant, large package of extra fine, Assorted Ribbons (by mail), in different widths and all the latest fashionable shades ; adapted for Bonnet Strings, Neckwear, Scarfs, Trimming for Hats and Dresses, Bows, Fancy Work, &c., can get an astonishing big bargain, owing to the recent failure of a large wholesale Ribbon Manufacturing Co., by sending only 25c. (stamps), to the address we give below.

As a *special offer*, this house will give *double* the amount of any other firm in America if you will send the names and P.O. address of ten *newly* married ladies when ordering and mention the name of this paper. No pieces less than one yard in length. Satisfaction guaranteed, or money cheerfully refunded. Three packages for 60 cents. Address,
LONDON RIBBON AGENCY,
JERSEY CITY, N.J.

The *Mohawk Standard* charges Henry Hechler with selling to Dr. Fraser restrikes of the Halifax Ferry Tokens, for genuine.

Batchelder Postage Stamp Company,

2006 GRAND AV., ST. LOUIS, MO., U.S.

WHOLESALE PRICE LIST

These prices are made to dealers only. Orders under $1.00 respectfully declined.
Wholesale list sent free on application.

UNUSED STAMPS.

	Per 10	Per 100
Allen's Locals, red or yellow...	10	75

USED STAMPS.

Our selections of used stamps are guaranteed to be far superior to any other wholesale dealers. We will at all times guarantee our patrons fine mixtures. If in some instances our prices are a little higher, the mixture is enough better to pay for the addition in prices.

Country	Per 10	Per 100
Argentine Republic, well assorted $0 10		$0 75
Austria, well assorted..............................		15
Austrian Italy, well assorted	07	50
Azores, well assorted........................	15	
Baden, " "	10	70
Barbados " "	06	35
Bermuda " "	12	1 00
Brazil " "	07	40
Bolivia " "	35	
Bosnia " "	15	1 00
Br. Guiana " "		25
Bulgaria " "	10	80
Cape of Good Hope, well assorted..............		30
Central America, finely assorted.................		1 50
Ceylon, 74, 2c....................................	10	
" 2, 4 and 8c..........................		60
" 5c...................................		25
" 5c. on 8c..........................	10	75
" 5c. on 64c........................1	00	
Chili, 5c. assorted................................		25
Costa Rica, 1c., green......	10	
" " 2c., red..........................	15	
Cuba, 1857	10	
" 1864, green ane pink assorted	20	
" 1869, 10c. brown....................	12	
" 1870, 10c. green....................	12	
" 1871, 25c. blue....................	12	
" 1873, 25c., lilac	15	
" well mixed, 57-82....................		60
Cyprus, ½p, green	10	70
Denmark, assorted..............................		10
Dominican Republic, 1885....................	20	
Eastern Roumelia, well assorted	15	
Ecuador, 5c., blue..............................	10	80
Egypt, well assorted..............................		50
Finland, " "		25
France, 77, 30-40-75c., 1f......................		40
Greece, well assorted..............................		25
Hong Kong, well assorted......................	12	1 00
Honduras, " "	15	1 30
Iceland, 10a	20	
India, well assorted..............................		25
Italy, segnatasse well assorted...........	05	30
India, H. M. S., assorted		20
Jamaica, well assorted		30
Japan, " "	06	40
" 2c, red..........................		25
Mauritius, 79, 4c..............................	10	
" 80, 2c.	15	
Mexico, 1874, 5c., brown......................	20	1 75
" 1874, 25c	07	60
" 1875, 50c., green....................	50	
" 2878, 10, orange....................	10	1 00
" 1880, 4c	80	7 00
" 1879, 5c. orange	10	
" 1879, 10c. blue....................	15	
" 1884, 1c. green....................	08	75
" 2c., green..........................	10	1 00
" 3. green	20	1 70
" 4c "	15	
" 6c "	30	
" 10c "	03	

Country	Per 10	Per 100
" " 20c "	30	
" " 25c green	50	
" " well assorted		90
" 1885, 2c., rose..........................	15	
" " 3c., brown	25	2 00
" " 4c., salmon, ...	60	5 00
" " 5c., blue	15	
" " 6c., brown..........................	25	2 00
" " 10c., orange	15	
" " well assorted		1 20
" 1886, 1c., green, ...	08	60
" " 2c., rose, ...	10	90
" " 3c., lilac	12	1 00
" " 4c., lilac	20	
" " 5c., blue	08	75
" " 6c	15	
" " 10c. lilac	07	65
" Official, 1886, red..........................	35	2 00
Natal, 1874, 1p, carmine	05	40
" well assorted, no 1p	20	
Norway, finely assorted, ...		20
New South Wales, 1p and 2p		20
New Zealand, 1p and 2p..........................		20
Persia, well assorted	20	1 75
Portugal " "		20
Porto Rico, 4 var. 25 surcharg'd..............	20	1 75
Porto Rico, 1876 surcharged cross paraph...	30	
" 25, blue 1877	06	50
" 1898, 25c., green	06	40
" 1879, 25c..........................	07	
" 1882, 1c., green	07	
" 2m., purple	07	
Porto Rico, 5c., blue	04	25
" well assorted		40
Queensland, assorted..............................		20
Roumania, well assorted..........................		20
Russia..		15
South Australia, 1p and 2p......................		20
Servia, well assorted..............................		50
Spain, " "		15
Spain, war, well assorted..........................		15
Straits Settlements, well ass't'd.....	12	
Switzerland, well assorted......................		10
Tasmania, " "		25
Trinidad, assorted..............................		10
Turkey, well ass'td, old and new		50
United States of Columbia, astd..............	10	
Venezuela, assorted..............................	10	
Victoria, "	08	30
Western Australia, 1p and 2p	07	45
United States, Postoffice, 3c	05	35
" " Interior, 3c..........................	06	40
" " Treasury, 3 and 6c......................	10	90
" " 6 var.		2 00
" " War, 3c..........................	15	1 00
" " 2c..........................	15	1 00
" " 3 and 6c..........................		70
" " envelopes		60
" " Locals, well ass'td		1 25
" " Centennial, 3c., green and red...		1 25
" " Agriculture.............	30	

(Continued from preceding page.)

Well Mixed—Suitable for Sheets.

	Per 10	Per 100		Per 10	Per 100
To sell at 1c. each....................................		30	To sell at 4 and 5c. each...........................	20	1 50
" " " 2c. "	10	60	" " " 8 to 10c. "	40	3 50
" " " 3c. "	12	1 00			

Well Assorted Continentals.

10,000..........................$1 75 ; 25,000..$3 00 ; 100,000 ....$10 00

Blank Approval Sheets.

Ruled in two colors to hold 40 stamps. Sample free. Prices: 25 for 15c ; 50, 25c; 100 50c ; 500, $2. Sent post free on receipt of price.

YOUNG AMERICAN POSTAGE STAMP ALBUM.

Contains space for 2000 stamps.

This book fills a want long felt by beginners, who wish a cheap book, or for those who wish a cheap book to put in their duplicates. Stamp-issuing countries in alphabetical order. Plenty of room for all new issues. The best, cheapest and handsomest book ever made for the price. Price 25 cents. By mail 28 cents. This book contains some novel features never before introduced.

HALF DIME SETS.

The left-hand figure denotes the number of varieties in each set. Price 5c. a set. Five sets 25c., 12 sets 50c. or the entire lot, 61 sets, containing 310 stamps, sent post free for $2.65.

To every person purchasing the entire lot we will give a Triangle Newfoundland stamp. This stamp retails for 25c.

5 Argentine.	2 Monaco.	4 Egypt.	4 Tasmania.	4 Peru.
4 Austria and Italy.	5 Porto Rico.	5 Finland.	3 Trinidad.	8 Russia.
10 Austria.	7 Portugal.	10 France.	2 Grenada.	3 Venezuela.
8 Australia.	4 Prussia.	3 French Colonies.	5 Greece.	5 Victoria.
3 Bermuda.	9 Russia.	10 Denmark.	10 Holland.	8 Wurtemberg.
4 Barbados.	5 Sardinia.	5 Sardinia.	10 Great Britain	10 U.S. Postage.
4 Baden.	3 Straits Settlements.	3 Sandwich Isles.	3 Hong Kong.	10 U.S. Envelope.
3 Bulgaria.	4 Ceylon.	5 Servia.	1 Iceland.	5 U.S. Departments.
5 Brazil.	2 Confederate	10 Spain.	5 India.	4 U.S. War.
5 Bosnia.	2 Cyprus.	8 Sweden.	2 Italy.	3 Hamburg.
5 Chili.	5 Cape of Good Hope.	4 Sweden Official.	4 Jamaica.	
7 Canada.	4 Cuba	10 Swiss.	4 Japan.	
6 Mexico.	3 Dutch Indies.	5 Turkey.	5 Luxemburg.	

DIME SETS.

The left hand figure denotes the number of varieties in each set. Price 10 cents a set, 5 sets for 50 cents, 11 sets for $1.00 or the entire lot of 73 sets containing 457 stamps sent post free for $6.35.

To any person purchasing the entire lot we will give an Argentine Republic 60 cents stamp. This stamp retails for 50c.

15 Australian.	5 Bulgaria.	4 France unpaid.	10 Porto Rico.	8 Victoria.
3 Alsace and Loraine.	7 Brazil.	6 French Colonies.	5 Orange States.	8 U.S. Officials.
3 Angola.	4 Isr. Guiana.	7 Finland.	3 Paraguay.	15 U.S Revenues.
7 Argentine Republic.	10 Canada	16 Great Britain.	2 Fiji Isles.	5 U.S. of Columbia.
20 Austria.	8 Canada Bill.	4 Guatemala.	7 Peru.	3 Trinidad.
6 Austria and Italy.	3 Canada Law.	7 Greece.	5 Servia.	6 Sweden Losen.
4 Azores.	7 Cape of Good Hope.	3 Hayti.	17 Spain.	6 Sweden Official
6 Baden.	6 Ceylon.	5 Hong Kong.	5 Sandwich Isles.	2 Philippine Isles.
7 Barbados.	6 Chili.	4 Heligoland.	5 Saxony.	3 Nicaragua.
5 Bergedorf.	2 Persia.	7 Japan.	8 Roman States.	4 Natal.
7 Bavaria.	2 Congo.	8 Jamaica.	7 Roumania.	5 Ecuador.
6 Bavaria Return Letter	7 Cuba.	10 India.	6 Turkey.	
3 Bahamas.	4 Eastern Roumelia.	10 Mexico.	2 Simoor.	
4 Bermuda.	7 Egypt.	4 Monaco.	5 Straits Settlements.	
5 Bosnia.	20 France.	4 Newfoundland.	5 Venezuela.	

Special attention is called to the above 5 and 10 cent sets. The stamps are all guaranteed genuine and if desired a written guarantee will be sent with each order. Your attention is called to the number of varieties in each set and and if the same stamps were to be sold single they would bring twice as much as we get for them when put up in sets.

BARGAINS
GOOD TILL JULY 15TH

4 var. Persia Official, 1881..........	$0 15	7 " Bulgaria		10
15 " Mexico................	15	1 " 1c. U.S. Periodical.........		15
15 " Porto Rico	20	6 " Mexico Porte D. Mar, colored		31
2 " Mexico ruled paper........	25			
25 " Mexico	50	United States Interior—complete set		1 50
40 " Mexico	1 00	" " State " "		5 00
3 " Salvador, 1867...........	10	" " Post Office " "		2 00
5 " Guatemela, 1882, unused	10	" " War " "		75
4 " Nicaragua unused	40	All above unused.		

JULY-AUGUST   1888.

Toronto
Philatelic Journal

A Monthly Magazine
For Stamp Collectors

NORTH
AMERICA

SOUTH
AMERICA

TORONTO PHILATELIC CO
106 HURON STREET.

TORONTO CANADA.

TOR. ENG. CO.

Toronto Philatelic Journal.

OFFICIAL ORGAN OF CANADIAN PHILATELIC ASSOCIATION.

VOL. 3   TORONTO, JULY, 1888.   No. 1.

SAVED FROM THE HAMMER.

BY JULIA S. MASON.

The day was drawing to a close one of those glorious June days, the pride of our Canadian summer ; the sun was just sinking. behind the tall steeple of a neighboring church, but before bidding adieu to the busy city it sent a soft kindly ray through the latticed window of a lowly looking cottage, and rested on the flushed and wasted features of a little girl, apparently about 9 years of age, whom we will introduce to our readers as Ella Linden. Beside the bed stood a tall dignified looking lady with handsome features, but whose face was sadly marred with mental suffering. As she bent over the little sufferer a stranger could easily read in the careworn affectionate face the relationship that existed between nurse and patent, Mrs. Linden, for she was the child's mother, looked like a person who had seen better days. In fact, she had been reared in comparative luxury.

In order to give our readers a brief history of the interesting personages who form our brief sketch we will have to go back a few years. Two brothers,· Edgar and Walter Linden, had been left orphans. In England provision had been made for their maintenance and education. Rev. Mr. Lockwood who had been appointed their guardian, and who had been an intimate friend of their parents, spared no pains in giving the boys a good English education. While their holidays were spent at his house their companion and playmate a lovely little girl who was under the tutelage of a resident governess. Many happy days were spent with her new found companions during vacation roaming over the commons and through wooded grove under the care of her governess in search of botanical specimens. Her companions were intense lovers of nature, and many were the specimens of insect life which found their way into Mr. Lockwood's library where he had prepared cabinets for their reception. Thus developing a practical knowledge of the natural sciences that could not otherwise be obtained. But when the weather rendered those out-door amusements impracticable their chief pleasure consisted in philatelic research. In this Mr. Lockwood lent his encouragement for well he knew that in this occupation they would combine valuable knowledge with amusement, and ever on the alert to develop the minds of his beloved charge; he allowed them to devote a part of their pocket money in purchasing the postage· stamps of the· different counties and assisting them in learning the history and data of each. They proved apt pupils and in time amassed a mind of general knowledge as well as a magnificent collection of revenue stamps which was in itself of no mean value. On arriving at manhood Edgar took his portion of his father's fortune and sought the far famed shores of New Zealand, where he hoped to increase his fortune by careful investment. Walter remained with his guardian who placed him in business, where by careful and prompt attention he soon became an expert in his branch of trade. In course of time he loved and won the hand of Miss Lockwood, his guardian's daughter, and with bright prospects and anticipations came to Canada, determined to try his fortune in the new world. He opened up business in one of our commercial cities. Two children, a boy and girl blest their union. For a time all went well; prosperity seemed to be their lot until he overstepped the bounds of prudence and in an unlucky moment ventured in speculation, which proved disastrous to his business. As usual in such cases the worst came, and poor Mr. Linden after satisfying his creditors found he had nothing left. A friend in kindly sympathy offered him a position in his warehouse which he gladly accepted in order to provide for the immediate wants of his family. In his heroic attempts to build up his fallen fortunes he made undue demands on his strength. With a mind ill at ease and an overworked body he soon fell a victim to disease. While returning home one evening from business, exhausted both in mind and body, a cold and heavy rain storm swept up, and before he could reach the car, was thoroughly saturated. The long ride home produced a chill which resulted in pneumonia. The morning found him delirious. He rallied but a few days, and then the end came as it comes to us all, but to him in the full vigor of youth it came all too soon. But what wonder it is when we reflect how business men spend their days in the anxiety for wealth, in the bustle, the jostle, the rush and excitement, combined with hurried meals and close impure offices, the wonder is that so many survive. Mrs. Linden now felt the keen edge of sorrow. What woman who has passed through the same but knows the utter wretchedness the fierce heartache. But for her children's sake she must not nurse her grief. They have no one to look to now for protection and support but herself, for, since her husband's failure, her friends had lost sight of her. These shots pass rapidly through her mind as she sits behind him who was once beautiful in life now to her beautiful even in death. She could gaze on that pale refined face and see a hollowed smile resting on the half parted lips. Softly her children creep into the chamber of death and with their artless questions innocently bring their mother out of her lethergic grief. After the last said rites had been paid to the departed, Mrs. Linden realized for the first time in her life what it was to face the world, and earn her own and her children's bread. But one thing her mind was fixed on, she would never give up her children. They would never be without a mother's love and care while she had life. With this firm resolve and blessed with good health and a large amount of courage, she went forward taking up the burden of life, and to a lady of her refined sensibility and tender training it was no easy task, but she had a vigorous intellect and thanks to her father's prudent training her mind had been stored with a large fund of useful knowledge which she turned to practical account in lessening the expenses and rendering her home comfortable. We will not follow her into the details of her life, her struggles and heartaches. She met with many obstacles but occasionally some encouraging circumstance would produce a silver lining on her otherwise obscure horizon. She selected a small but neatly appointed cottage in a respectable quarter of the city. She was skilled in fine art and needle work, also drawing and music. She also possessed a fine rich voice which she now prized and valued as it would be a means of contributing to the comfort of her little ones. With a brave heart and undaunted courage she soon found open avenues for her talents. A position was obtained in one of the large church choirs, and this soon led to a recognition of her musical talents. Her services soon became in great demand.

(TO BE CONTINUED.)

More About Miss Green.

The Miss Green swindle has now become quite interesting, and additional developments are coming to light. This party was in Winnipeg on April last, and wrote to Mr. W. B. Hale, of Williamsville. Mass., as Miss Ada Krinington. giving the fictitious reference of McKay & Bland, 214 Main St. Miss Krinington said her uncle was postmaster at Toronto 25 years ago(?) The postmaster at Winnipeg wrote to say that there are no such persons as McKay and Bland, and that Miss Ada Krinington had left there in May or June. She next turned up at Lincoln. Neb., as Miss Etta F. King, giving writing reference from " Strong & Co." From there she went to Denton, which is in same county as Lincoln. There she wrote under the name of Miss Jessie E. Green, giving reference of J. G. McKay and J. J. Winters, barrister. Next we hear of her at Los Angeles, where Alec M. Krinington is the name used. Further developments in this wonderful case are expected and anything relating to it should be sent to John R. Hooper. Vice-President, C.P.A.. Ottawa, Ont.. who has sifted the case to the bottom. This bogus female is being tracked by a U.S. P.O. Inspector for swindling through the mails, while the chief detective of 'Minneapolis police department. has the case in his hands with orders to arrest for robbery. Already over $300 in stamps is known to have been sent to this king of frauds. Here is a chance surely for the A.P.A. or some other society to distinguish itself by taking this case in hand.

———

ROME, N.Y.. July 7th, 1888.

GENTLEMEN,—I noticed your charges against Miss Jessie E. Green, of Denton, Neb., in the June No. of the TORONTO PHILATELIC JOURNAL, and having a small amount invested in Miss Green, I write you not for sympathy and condolence, but to show you the recommendation given by her to me, endorsed by J. J. Winters, Jr. I have made no enquiry in regard to her as my investment in her is small," not to exceed $5.50, and shall await the result of your investigation.

Yours very truly,
C. E. FRASER.

———

DENTON, NEB., Feb. 25th, 1888.
Mr. C. E. Fraser, Jr.,
Lee Center, N.Y., Box 4.

Dear Sir,—I am an agent here for stamps, coins and curiosities and can sell a great many of each, especially, coins, Could you send me a list of coins on approval? I can sell those worth from 10 to 30 cents each best.

Could also use to advantage a sheet of RARE U.S. stamps and a sheet of foreign, worth from 8 to 15 cents each.

Below is my written reference. Can furnish more if this is not enough.

Yours respectfully,
MISS JESSIE E. GREEN,
Denton, Neb., Lancaster Co.

Miss Jessie E. Green is perfectly reliable and in every way worthy of your trust.

J. J. WINTERS, JR.,
Attorney-at-law.

———

If you have not seen Townsend's Philatelic Directory send 25 cents and receive one. George A. Lowe, 106 Huron Street, Toronto, agent for Canada.

TORONTO
ᑭHILᗩTELIᏟ ᒍOUᖇNᗩL.

Published on the 1st of every month.

Geo. A. Lowe,   **Jos . Hooper,**
Ed. Philatelic Deft.   Ed. Numismatic Dept·

SUBSCRITION :
United States and Canada 35c. per year ; Foreign Countries,
50c. per year.

Advertising Rates :

1 inch	0 50
2 "	0 80
½ column	1 50
1 "	2 50
1 page	4 50

10 per cent. discount on standing advts.

Copy wanted not later than the 25th.
Remit money by P.O. order, or small amounts in one or
two cent stamps.
Address all correspondence to the

Toronto Philatelic Co.
06 Huron St.   **Toronto, Canada.**

TORONTO, JULY-AUGUST, 1888.

At a meeting of philatelists held in this
city on the 9th inst. it was decided to
form a joint stock company for the publication of albums, standard catalogues, etc.
The publishing business of Geo. A. Lowe,
including the TORONTO PHILATELIC JOUR-
NAL, has been taken over by the company,
which will, beginning with September
number, enlarge and increase the circulation. The following are parties who have
subscribed shares up to time of going to
press :

T. J. McMinn, Toronto ; H. Morell, To-
ronto ; E. J. Rogerson, Barrie ; F. J.
Grenny, Brantford ; Mrs.Mason, Toronto ;
H. E. French, Niagara Falls South ; F.
Ineson, Carlton West ; C. Wesley Price,
Paymouth, Mich.; J. C. Niesser, Toronto ;
Geo. A. Lowe. Toronto ; H. S. Harte,
Petitcodiac ; E. F. Wurtele, Quebec.

Parties desirous of taking stock in the
above, or for any information, address
        Geo. A. Lowe, *Sec. pro tem.*,
            106 Huron St., Toronto.

The Secretary of C.P.A. is now prepared to receive nominations for officers for
the ensuing year. The Toronto Branch
has issued the following ticket :

President, E. Y. Parker, Toronto.

Vice-President, Ontario.— Geo.Walker,
Peterboro.

Vice-President, N. S. — A. J. Craig,
Pictou.

Vice-President, Quebec.—R.A.B.Hart,
Montreal.

Vice-President, N. B.—H. S. Harte,
Petitcodiac.

Vice-President, P. E. I.--W. Brown,
Charlottetown.

Vice-President, B. C. — J. H. Todd,
Banff.

Secretary.—Geo. A. Lowe, Toronto.

Treasurer.—H L. Hart, Halifax.

Exchange Supt.—F. J. Grenny, Brantford.

Librarian.—J.A. Leighton, Orangeville.

Counterfeit Detector.—H. Morell, Toronto.

Purchasing Agent.—F. C. Kaye, Halifax.

Official Editor.—T. J. McMinn, Toronto.

Official Organ.—Toronto Philatelic
Journal

Executive Committee.—J. C. Niesser,
Toronto ; C. C. Morency, Quebec ; F.
C. Kaye, Halifax.

Convention 1889.– Montreal.

The election of officers will take place
at the Convention to be held in Toronto
on Sept. 19th and 20th. All members
who cannot attend, but wish to be represented. should send their proxies to
Mr. E. Y. Parker, 47 Huron St., Toronto,
with instructions as to how they wish
their vote to be cast. etc Members en-
trusting their provies to Mr. Parker can
be assured that their vote will be cast as
desired.

C.P.A.

SECRETARY'S REPORT.

Our list of applications this month shows a considerable falling off, which is, no doubt, due to the approach of the hot weather. I would again call the attention of those not having as yet joined our ranks to the fact that members are admitted for the balance of the year at 50c. No 40 was through an oversight published last month as having been expelled for non-payment of dues. This should *not* have been done, and I trust the gentleman will kindly overlook the error. Particulars of the Philatelic Exhibition to be held at our Convention next autumn will be found in another column, and I trust that as the time for preparation is very much limited, every member will put his shoulder to the wheel and labor earnestly to make the exhibit a success.

LIST OF APPLICATIONS, No. 4.

A. Lehmann, Jr., 635 Main Street, Paterson, N. J. Reference A.P.A.

A. T. Ogilvie, care A. W. Ogilvie & Co., Montreal, P.Q. Reference A. E. Labelle, H. F. Ketcheson.

Edw. C. Biggar, Fremont, Neb. References, Geo. A. Lowe, W. H Jones.

W. A. DeWolf Smith, New Westminster, B.C. References, A. W. Smith, S. DeWolf.

J. A. LEIGHTON,
Secy.

PRESIDENT'S REPORT.

To the Members of the C.P.A.:

GENTLEMEN,—After carresponding with and having the opinion of most of the officers and some of the members of our Association, I have decided that Toronto would be the most convenient place of meeting, and we will therefore meet there for our Annual Convention on September 19th and 20th.

I trust all the officers will be present, and as many of the members as possible, as many important matters will come before the meeting. Every member in good standing who cannot attend in person should make arrangements to be represented by proxy, which should be done in writing and signed before a witness.

I have been asked by some of the members about a stamp exhibition at same time as Convention, but think we had better wait till next year. It would be a good idea for all the members who attend to bring their collections with them.

As the election of officers will take place at Convention, the Secretary is now ready to receive nominations for the various offices to be filled.

The Constitution and By-laws will come before the meeting for amending and revising so we can have them printed and circulated among the members.

I trust the Toronto members will make all necessary arrangements for place of meeting, etc. .

Our Association is steadily growing and I want every member to secure at least one new member from among his fellow-collectors before the end of this year; I wish to double the membership and in order to do so will want the united help of the Association. We hope, by the beginning of next year, to have all the departments in working order.

Yours truly,
H. F. KETCHESON,
Pres. C.P.A.

DEAR SIR,— Since writing my official report I have reconsidered the question about a stamp exhibition, and have decided that we shall have one.

I will therefore name the following Executive Committee to make all necessary arrangements for said Exhibition: E. Y. Parker, T. J. McMinn, Geo. A. Lowe, J. A. Leighton, F. J. Grenny, and the following General Committee to collect and forward the exhibits to the Executive Committee: Williston Brown, P.E.I.; H. S. Harte, N.B.; J. A. Craig and J. Noble Crane, N.S.; C. C. Morency and R. A. Baldwin Hart, Quebec; J. R. Hooper, W. D. B. Spry, A. G. Needham, Mrs. Mason, Ontario; J. H. Todd, Manitoba and British Columbia ; J. M. Sheridan, Brooklyn, N.Y., for the U.S.

I trust all the members I have named on the General Committee will act and do all they can to make this exhibition a success.

H. F. KETCHESON.

EXCHANGE SUPT.'S REPORT.

The Exchange Department is very active, and a large number of stamps keep coming in. Send all you can, as a large variety of sheets gives me a better chance to suit the members' requirements. During the months of July and August a good many collectors are away or going away from home to spend their holidays, and stamp business generally languishes except with those ardent and enthusiastic philatelists whose numbers are on the increase —therefore, until September I will not send out as many books on circuit as usual. About sixty members are now taking advantage of the benefit derived from the exchange. Any member who has no duplicates to trade, but desires to obtain stamps from the Exchange Books, can do so, by notifying me. Two branches are now in operation. No. of sheets received filled to date 350, value—$1,500.

F. J. GRENNY,
Ex. Supt.

Philatelic Literature.

Send list of wants and prices paid for same. 50 stamps for every stamp paper sent me. Correspondence solicited for the exchange of Philatelic Papers. The Philatelic Literature Collector, 10 cents a year. Stamps on approval at 25% off Scott on receipt of good reference. Complete file stamp Record, 4 numbers, 25c.

H. C. BEARDSLEY, C. P. A. 38,
422 N. 7th St., St. Joseph, Mo.
c. cash for any number of vol. 12 of American Journal of Philately.

OLD SPANISH,
—AND—
Montezuma, Aztec Relics, Indian Pottery, Moccasins, Suits, Spears, Bows, Gods, Drums,

And other articles too numerous to mention. Send for circular. Would like to exchange goods for advertisement.
Yours, etc.,
N. M. NORFLEET,

ANNOUNCEMENT.

The undersigned beg to inform the philatelic public that he has purchased the *Canadian Philatelist*, and will continue its publication in a new form. The size of page will be 3 columns each, 11 inches long, and will commence with Vol. II. for convenience of binding, etc.

A guaranteed circulation of **4000** copies monthly.

SUBSCRIPTION PER YEAR:

To Canada and United States free; Great Britain, 6 cents; other countries, 12 cents.

ADVERTISING RATES:

1 inch	$ 35	1 column, 11 in	$2 35
⅓ "	75	1 page, 33 "	6 25
½ col.	1 35		

Rates will be advanced 25%. Make your contracts now. Dealers, send a trial adv. and remember the large circulation.

Send your address on a post card and secure No. 1. which will be out about Sept. 1st, 1888.
Send copy at once to.

H. E. FRENCH,
Member of C.P.A. Box 60, Niagara Falls South, Ont.

LOOK HERE!

10,000 Canadian 1c. and 3c. Stamps

PILED NICELY IN HUNDREDS.

Also 1,000 2c. Registers, 4,000 Bill stamps — 14 varieties.

Will sell the above for best offer either cash or exchange.

GEO. A. LOWE,
106 HURON ST.,
TORONTO, CANADA.

Items.

Additional facts are coming to light regarding the approval sheet stealing which has been carried on at Denton, Neb., by a young man who goes by the name of *Miss* Jessie E. Greene. Not only have Canadians suffered but dozens of dealers in the U.S., including the proprietor of the *Mohawk Standard* and Mr. Wm. B. Hall, of Williamsville, Mass. The later states he has been defrauded by this party,.and that. he has placed the matter in the hands of the trustees of the A.P.A.

Mr. Hechler will be a candidate for the Presidency of the C.P.A. at the next election.

Rev. Henry S. Harte, who is one of the best informed philatelists in the Maritime Provinces, is getting out a sketch of Canada's fiscal stamps.

NUMISMATIC DEPARTMENT.

All matters relating to this department should be addressed to Jos. Hooper, Box 145 Port Hope, Ont.

We have received a full set of Canadian Silver for 1888—50c. piece, 25c., 10c. and 5c., also the " Copper cent," same date.

The Bank of Montreal, side view, half penny, 1838 (in very fine condition) realized $32.50 at the W. N. Friesner sale held in Philadelphia, April 5th and 6th last.

The demand for Canadian coin still prevails, and the collectors are increasing in number ; greater enthusiasm apparently prevails in the Province of Quebec than any of the other portions of the Dominion.

We recently sold No. 23 (Leroux) at $7.50 cash. No. 47 has been enquired for by several advanced collectors lately and and is difficult to procure. We recently obtained the 50c. Brit Coloniar as Leroux No. 74. No. 85, Jamaica on Barrel, is another extreme rarity, and hard to find.

The following is a description of a bronze Jubilee Medal, 1887, just received from England. Size, 49. Obverse, veiled bust of the Queen Victoria ; around circle "VictoriaRegina et Imperatrix." Reverse, in the centre a figure representing the British Empire sits enthroned, with the sea in the background, resting one hand on the sword of justice, and holding in the other the spmbol of victorious rule. A lion is seen on each side of the throne. At the feet of the seated figure lies Mercury, the God of Commerce, the mainstay of our imperial strength, holding up in one hand a cup heaped with gold. Opposite to him sits the Genius of Electricity and Steam. Below, again, five shields banded together bear the names of the five parts of the globe, Europe, Asia, Africa, America and Australia, over which the Empire extends. On each side of the figure of Empire stand the personified elements of its greatness--on the right (of the spectator) Industry and Agriculture ; on the left, Science, Letters, and Art. Above, the occasion of the celebration commemorated is expressed by two winged figures representing the years 1887 (the advancing figure), and the year 1837 (with averted head),holding each a wreath. Where these wreaths interlock, the letters V. R. I. appear, and over all the words " In Commemoration."

Dr. Leroux's new work has been received. Its title " The Canadian Coin Cabinet " (price $5). While it represents considerable labor in its compilation, and in numbers run to 1881, still it falls far short of what is desired ; many interesting pieces have been left out. The engraving of about one-half is mediocre, and the interesting description as given in McLachlan's work of each piece is altogether left out. The metal varieties are not given, and were, we expected and looked for, an interesting and fully illustrated and correct illustration of Sous. The engravings are so poor as to be in many cases unintelligible. A full compendium and correct list of Canadian coins, medals and tokens remains still a work of the future; we know of no one so able to produce such a useful work as Robt. W. McLachlan, Esq., of Montreal, and look forward with great expectancy to his supplementary work. The manuscript for which is well prepared, and will, we are promised, be issued this fall. While we do not wish to disparage the Dr.'s effort to give us all he was able, and would give him credit for work accomplished, still we have to state that a more thorough work, well described and fully illustrated, will yet be written and completed out of the material already furnished, together with more lucid descriptions, a better class of engravings and more systemization in arrangement. A very voluminous manuscript by Gerald E. Hart, Esq., of Montreal, which the editor of this department had the pleasure of examining would furnish valuable material which is yet wanted, and we hope to see utilized.

SILK RIBBONS.

Those of our lady readers who wou'd like to have an elegant, large package of extra fine Assorted Ribbons (by mail), in different widths and all the latest fashionable shades : adapted for Bonnet Strings, Neckwear, Scarfs, Trimming for Hats and Dresses, Bows, Fancy Works. &c., can get an astonishing big bargain, owing to the recent failure of a large wholesale Ribbon Manufacturing Co., by sending only 25c. (stamps), to the address we give below.

As a *special offer*, this house will give *double* the amount of any other firm in America if you will send the names and P.O. address of ten *newly* married ladies when ordering and mention the name of this paper. No pieces less than one yard in length. Satisfaction guaranteed

or money cheerfully refunded. Three packages for 60 cents. Address,
LONDON RIBBON AGENCY,
JERSEY CITY, N.J.

Lightning Source UK Ltd.
Milton Keynes UK
UKHW010950061118
331795UK00007B/423/P